GLOBALIZATION
AND MIGRATION

GLOBALIZATION

Series Editors

Manfred B. Steger

*Royal Melbourne Institute of Technology
and University of Hawai'i–Ma⁻noa*

and

Terrell Carver

University of Bristol

"Globalization" has become *the* buzzword of our time. But what does it mean? Rather than forcing a complicated social phenomenon into a single analytical framework, this series seeks to present globalization as a multidimensional process constituted by complex, often contradictory interactions of global, regional, and local aspects of social life. Since conventional disciplinary borders and lines of demarcation are losing their old rationales in a globalizing world, authors in this series apply an interdisciplinary framework to the study of globalization. In short, the main purpose and objective of this series is to support subject-specific inquiries into the dynamics and effects of contemporary globalization and its varying impacts across, between, and within societies.

Supported by the Globalization Research Center at the University of Hawai'i, Mānoa

GLOBALIZATION AND MIGRATION

A WORLD IN MOTION

ELIOT DICKINSON

ROWMAN & LITTLEFIELD
Lanham • Boulder • New York • London

Published by Rowman & Littlefield
A wholly owned subsidiary of The Rowman & Littlefield Publishing Group, Inc.
4501 Forbes Boulevard, Suite 200, Lanham, Maryland 20706
www.rowman.com

Unit A, Whitacre Mews, 26-34 Stannary Street, London SE11 4AB, United Kingdom

British Library Cataloguing in Publication Information Available

Library of Congress Cataloging-in-Publication Data
Names: Dickinson, Eliot, author.
Title: Globalization and migration : a world in motion / Eliot Dickinson.
Description: Lanham : Rowman & Littlefield, [2016] | Series: Globalization |
    Includes bibliographical references and index.
Identifiers: LCCN 2016005015 (print) | LCCN 2016017223 (ebook) | ISBN
    9781442254961 (cloth : alk. paper) | ISBN 9781442254978 (pbk. : alk.
    paper) | ISBN 9781442254985 (electronic)
Subjects: LCSH: Emigration and immigration. | Emigration and
    immigration—Economic aspects. | Globalization. | Globalization—Economic
    aspects.
Classification: LCC JZ1318 .D536 2016 (print) | LCC JZ1318 (ebook) | DDC
    304.8—dc23
LC record available at https://lccn.loc.gov/2016005015

Printed in the United States of America

Für Barbara, meine geliebte Frau, die mit mir bis ans Ende der Welt gegangen ist und mich auf dem Camino des Lebens begleitet

CONTENTS

TABLES AND MAPS

Acknowledgments

I am greatly indebted to Dr. Wolfgang C. Müller, who so graciously extended an invitation to be a visiting scholar at the University of Vienna's Institut für Staatswissenschaft. His generous help in securing a research visa allowed me to spend a full year in the majestic capital of the Alpine Republic and to see firsthand the enormity of the ongoing refugee crisis in Europe.

Many thanks are due to my esteemed colleagues at Western Oregon University. Ed Dover, Mark Henkels, and Mary Pettenger supported my application for sabbatical leave and covered for me while I was gone. Mike McGlade, John Rector, Ram Sil, and Elizabeth Swedo read early drafts and excerpts of the manuscript and gave invaluable feedback. Comrade Dean Braa shared his considerable knowledge of world-systems theory and helped refine my conceptual approach to global migration. Ross Burkhart of Boise State University very kindly offered encouragement on both the manuscript and ideas presented at the annual conference of the Pacific Northwest Political Science Association. John W. Smith, who for years has been a trusted friend and mentor, made many insightful comments on the final draft.

Cheers to the entire Dickinson clan, especially my mother Marie, Neal, Paul, Mary, Lore, Chrissie, and Eryn. Heartfelt thanks also to Dieter and Christiana and our wonderful circle of friends in Vienna. My deepest gratitude ultimately goes to my wife Barbara, who has given me what I always wanted from this life, namely "to call myself beloved, to feel myself beloved on this earth."

LIST OF ABBREVIATIONS

CAFTA	Central American Free Trade Agreement
CIA	Central Intelligence Agency
COP	Conference of the Parties
ECJ	European Court of Justice
ECSC	European Coal and Steel Community
EEC	European Economic Community
EU	European Union
GDP	Gross Domestic Product
ILO	International Labor Organization
IMF	International Monetary Fund
IOM	International Organization for Migration
MNCs	Multinational Corporations
NAFTA	North American Free Trade Agreement
OAPEC	Organization of Arab Petroleum Exporting Countries
OECD	Organisation for Economic Co-operation and Development
PEGIDA	Patriotic Europeans Against the Islamization of the West (in German: Patriotische Europäer gegen die Islamisierung des Abendlandes)
SEA	Single European Act
SDGs	Sustainable Development Goals
UKIP	United Kingdom Independence Party
UN	United Nations
UNDP	United Nations Development Programme
UNEP	United Nations Environment Programme
UNESCO	United Nations Educational, Scientific and Cultural Organization
UNHCR	United Nations High Commissioner for Refugees

UNICEF	United Nations Children's Fund (formerly United Nations International Children's Emergency Fund)
UNRWA	United Nations Relief and Works Agency for Palestine Refugees
WTO	World Trade Organization

CHAPTER 1

THE ONSET OF A BORDERLESS WORLD

"This is the end of the road," said Ali Najaf, "I'm not going back."[1] The twenty-five-year-old ethnic Kurd from Syria had good reason to want to stay in Germany. He had cut short his studies to be a petroleum engineer in the besieged city of Homs when masked militants took him captive in the summer of 2013, interrogated him, and threatened to slit his throat. Fearing for his life, he fled with his mother, brother, and two sisters into neighboring Turkey and then into Bulgaria, the poorest member of the European Union, where he applied for political asylum. Facing hostility, prejudice, and generally miserable conditions in a crowded refugee camp, and knowing all the while that Germany promised more generous opportunities than Bulgaria, he paid a smuggler a fee of 235 euros per person—enough to cover travel expenses and bribes along the way—to drive him and his family north. After arriving at an asylum seeker processing center in Dortmund, Ali was resettled in the eastern German city of Eisenhüttenstadt to await a decision on his asylum status.

It is likely that Ali and his family will live in Europe for many years to come. There is little left for them in Syria, which has been devastated by years of civil war, ethnic conflict, and grinding poverty. The chances of staying permanently in Germany, where Ali's uncle already lives, are very good. The longer he stays and puts down roots, the less likely it is that he will leave and the more likely it is that he will integrate into society with the help of social networks associated with the already large Kurdish population in Germany. He is, after all, a bright and resourceful young man with an impressive command of English who wants an opportunity to go to university and, like everyone else, pursue his own happiness and live a beautiful life.

The Patriotic Europeans Against the Islamization of the West, a conservative group known by its German acronym "Pegida," however, have a different vision.[2] If they had their way, the Najafs would all be returned immediately to Bulgaria, which European Union asylum law says is a "safe third country." To Pegida, the Syrian family represents a threat to the traditional, prosperous, orderly way of life in Germany. What if Ali was a member of a Syrian militia group and not a student, as he claims? What if he brings the fight for Kurdish independence to the streets of Germany, or turns out to be a Muslim extremist, or worse, a terrorist? If Ali goes to university in Germany and gets a job, will it come at the expense of a German citizen? How much will it cost taxpayers to house, feed, and care for the Najafs and hundreds of thousands more asylum seekers like them?[3] If a court ever decides it is time for them to return home, will they voluntarily go or somehow manage to stay in Germany like so many others who defy their deportation orders?

Right wing groups across Europe felt vindicated when the brothers Saïd and Chérif Kouachi stormed the offices of the satirical newspaper *Charlie Hebdo* in Paris on January 7, 2015, yelling "God is Great!" and "We have avenged the Prophet Muhammad" before killing twelve people. To them it was evidence of out-of-control immigration from outside the so-called European cultural sphere, the failure to integrate immigrants and their children into society, and a realization of their fear that immigration poses a threat to national security. The leader of Pegida, Lutz Bachmann, said the attack in Paris was "further proof" justifying the existence of his organization.[4] Nigel Farage of the United Kingdom Independence Party (UKIP) told members of the European Parliament that Europe had "pursued policies of immigration at a rate that has made it frankly impossible for many new communities to integrate."[5] In France, right wing politician Marine Le Pen claimed "the massive waves of immigration, both legal and clandestine" that the country had experienced for decades had "prevented the implementation of a proper assimilation policy" and exacerbated the problem of unemployment.[6]

The nexus between migration and terrorism again reared its ugly head in Paris on the cool fall evening of Friday, November 13, 2015, when at least 130 people were killed in six coordinated attacks carried out by Islamic State militants. In the most deadly attack, four gunmen stormed into the Bataclan concert hall where the California band Eagles of Death Metal were playing to a sold-out crowd of 1,500 fans. Wielding massive Kalashnikov rifles and wearing suicide vests packed with explosives, they massacred eighty-nine people before blowing themselves up. According to one eyewitness account of the slaughter, one of the gunmen shouted at his victims, "you killed our brothers in Syria. We're here now," referring to France's military involvement in Syria and Iraq.[7] French president François Hollande responded to the blowback by stating that it was "an act of war" committed by "an army of Jihadists against France" and that the French response would be "ruthless."[8] Prime minister Manuel Valls warned of the danger of possible chemical and biological weapons attacks, and declared it was "a new kind of war, because borders are of no concern."[9] Complicating matters further were reports confirmed by French and Greek authorities that two of the dead terrorists had entered the European Union through Greece, where they had been registered as asylum seekers only six weeks earlier.[10]

These momentous events present a sampling of some of the most intriguing and complex dimensions of global migration. They offer a smorgasbord of timely topics—from war refugees, terrorism, population growth, and political asylum law to human rights, immigrant integration, ethnic conflict, and the challenge of border control—that are likely to remain on the global political agenda for the foreseeable future. The Office of the United Nations High Commissioner for Refugees (UNHCR) reminded us of this in June 2014 when it announced that the number of asylum seekers, refugees, and internally displaced people in the world had reached 51.2 million, the highest number since the end of World War II. "We are seeing here the immense costs of not ending wars, of failing to resolve or prevent conflict," and without vitally needed political solutions, said high commissioner António Guterres, "the alarming levels of conflict and the mass suffering that is reflected in these figures will continue."[11] Exactly a year later, on June 20, 2015 (World Refugee Day), the situation had only worsened as the number of forcibly displaced people rose to 59.5 million. "We have reached a moment of truth," the High Commissioner said. "World stability is falling apart leaving a wake of displacement on an unprecedented scale. Global powers have become either passive observers or distant players in the conflicts driving so many innocent civilians from their homes."[12]

THE MOST INTIMATE FORM OF GLOBALIZATION

Globalization is often thought of primarily in economic terms and defined, for instance, as "the development of an increasingly integrated global economy marked especially by free trade, free flow of capital, and the tapping of cheaper foreign labor markets."[13] Stated in broader but still concise terms, it is "the intensification of economic, political, social, and cultural relations across borders."[14] In its most eloquent expression it is simply "the compression of time and space,"[15] and the onset of a "borderless world."[16] As David Held and Anthony McGrew point out, globalization is a process (or set of processes) that involves the following types of change:

- It stretches social, political, and economic activities across political frontiers, regions, and continents.
- It intensifies our dependence on each other, as flows of trade, investment, finance, migration, and culture increase.
- It speeds up the world. New systems of transport and communication mean that ideas, goods, information, capital, and people move more quickly.
- It means that distant events have a deeper impact on our lives. Even the most local developments may come to have enormous global consequences. The boundaries between domestic matters and global affairs can become increasingly blurred.[17]

Examples of the blurring of global and local boundaries—referred to as glocalization—are abundant. When such things as economic crises, environmental catastrophes, political revolutions, terrorist attacks, or horrific wars unfold live on television and via the Internet, people feel affected even if they live thousands of miles away. When terrorists flew planes into the World Trade Towers in September 2001 or the popular uprising known as the Arab Spring swept across the Middle East and North Africa in 2011, people on all continents could see what was happening. When Typhoon Haiyan hit the Philippines in November 2013 or hundreds of thousands of refugees like the Najafs fled to Europe in 2015, they could talk about it on their cell phones, share their thoughts via email or Facebook and, if necessary, send money to friends, relatives, and others in need of help. Such events contribute to what scholars call "globality," a social consciousness in which people are aware of the many ways they are connected to their fellow human beings and the economic, political, cultural, and environmental interdependence of the planet.[18]

This book argues that the term globalization, which appeared in the 1960s and was popularized in the 1980s, describes a process that has been ongoing for more than five hundred years. It is linked to the sixteenth-century emergence of capitalism in Europe and the subsequent expansion of the capitalist world-system around the globe. As Immanuel Wallerstein puts it, globalization "is usually thought to refer to a reconfiguration of the world-economy that has only recently come into existence, in which the pressures on all governments to open their frontiers to the free movements of goods and capital is unusually strong . . . what is described as something new (relatively open frontiers) has in fact been a cyclical occurrence throughout the history of the modern world-system."[19] In relation to international migration, globalization is a dynamic process that has set the world in motion and incorporated millions of migrants into a global capitalist market whose dimensions are unprecedented in human history.

Migration literally means "to move from one place to another."[20] The root of the word, *migra*, comes from the Latin and is also found in the closely related words immigration (to enter, or in-migration), emigration (to depart, or out-migration), and remigration (to return, or return migration). Some scholars define migration broadly and place few restrictions on whether a person moves a long or short distance, within a country or across an international border, or why the move is made.[21] Such a broad definition is useful in a philosophical sense, for it helps us understand the basic concept of spatial mobility, but it can also be problematic because it casts such a wide net. At any given moment, billions of people are moving in all sorts of ways—from one side of town to the other, from rural to urban areas, from one state or province to the next, from one country to another, from the southern to the northern hemisphere, and so on. It is thus helpful to make distinctions between the major types of migration and categories of migrants.

The United Nations defines an international migrant as "anyone who changes his or her country of usual residence."[22] This standard definition applies to people who have crossed an international (external) border from one country to another, and excludes people migrating internally within their home country. Consequently, it leaves out one of the largest migrations in world history, namely the internal rural to urban migration of more than 140 million Chinese at the turn of the twenty-first century.[23] It also does not count the hundreds of millions of people who move within India, the United States, Indonesia, Russia, Brazil, and other large countries. While internal population movements are significant in their own right, they fall outside the scope of this study.

Distinguishing between short- and long-term international migration further helps us see the forest for the trees. A short-term international migrant is "a person who moves to a country other than his or her usual residence for a period of at least 3 months but less than a year (12 months) except in cases where the movement to that country is for purposes of recreation, holiday, visits to friends and relatives, business, medical treatment or religious pilgrimage."[24] In contrast, a long-term international migrant is "a person who moves to a country other than that of his or her usual residence for a period of at least a year (12 months), so that the country of destination effectively becomes his or her new country of residence."[25] While these distinctions may be slightly arbitrary given that there are many people on the cusp between long- and short-term, they provide a generally accepted way to classify migrants. It is long-term international migration that is of most interest here and to which I refer below.

Human beings are central to the process of globalization and are also the most important actors or "units of analysis" in migration.[26] Without people, neither globalization as we now know it nor human migration would occur. Without migrants spreading their various cultures, languages, religions, customs, ideas, and ways of life (not to mention diseases and prejudices), the course of world history most certainly would have evolved differently than it has. Thus, an important aspect of the relationship between globalization and migration—as opposed, for instance, to globalization and money, or globalization and democracy—is that it focuses on the lives of real human beings and not inanimate objects or theoretical abstractions. The hundreds of millions of migrants who are currently living outside their countries of origin are individuals with unique stories whose lives are not lived in isolation, but rather shared with the people around them. Their experiences are part of a larger human story, which affects us all. This, in large part, is why migration has been called "the most intimate form of globalization."[27]

According to the International Labor Organization (ILO), "most international migration today is related to seeking employment. More than 90 percent of all international migrants are workers and their families."[28] They are people from every corner of the globe and every conceivable walk of life. Some are highly skilled scientists, medical professionals, academics, artists, and athletes, while others are farm workers and manual laborers ready to make a living by any means necessary. They tend to be extraordinarily industrious and determined people who are prepared to do the dirty, difficult, and dangerous jobs—the so-called "Three-D Jobs"—that natives are either unwilling or unable to do. Approximately half are women, and one in seven is younger than twenty years old.[29] Many have been impoverished and dislocated by neoliberal economic policies that include a push toward privatization, deregulation, trade liberalization and tax cuts for the rich. In such cases migration becomes a matter of survival and leads to irregular, undocumented, or illegal migration, that is, people crossing international borders whether or not they have proper residence and work permits that allow them to lawfully enter and work in another country.

Hence, globalization and migration can each be viewed as separate processes, but it is hard to have a complete conversation about one without mentioning the other. In theory, you can have globalization without migration, and migration without globalization. In practice, though, the two spheres unavoidably overlap and are very much interconnected. Globalization causes migration, and migration contributes to the intensification of socioeconomic and political relations across borders. Taken together, the globalization of migration may be understood as "the tendency for more and more countries to be crucially affected by migratory movements at the same time."[30] As we shall see, migration can lead to the formation of harmonious multicultural societies, or it can create intense sectarian conflict and ethnic nationalist movements. Either way, the determinants of global migration inevitably involve questions of demography.

MIGRATION NATION

In *An Essay on the Principle of Population,* English demographer Thomas Robert Malthus (1766–1834) put forth the following postulates: "First, that food is necessary to the existence of man. Secondly, that the passion between the sexes is necessary, and will remain nearly in its present state."[31] He went on to argue that the global population would grow exponentially until it reached the earth's carrying capacity, or point at which there would not be enough food to feed everyone. This would lead to dire circumstances, including famine, disease, war, and forced migration. "A great emigration necessarily implies unhappiness of some kind or other in the country that is deserted," he wrote, "for few persons will leave their families, connections, friends, and native land, to seek a settlement in untried foreign climes, without some strong subsisting causes of uneasiness where they are, or the hope of some great advantages in the place to which they are going."[32] More than two centuries later, Malthus's arguments remain highly relevant as rapid population growth threatens to bring the earth to a tipping point marked by scarcity, deprivation, hunger, poverty, and environmental destruction.

The global population has been increasing at a phenomenal rate since it surpassed the one billion mark in 1804. In the twentieth century alone it tripled from two billion in 1930 to six billion in 1999. As illustrated in table 1.1, we are on schedule to hit 8.5 billion in 2030, 9.7 billion in 2050, and 11.2 billion by the end of the century.[33] This is significant because mass migration tends to increase along with the total world population. The number of international migrants grew from approximately 75 million in 1965 to 175 million in 2000 and, as shown in table 1.2, surpassed 220 million in 2010. By 2013 that number had risen to 232 million, which equaled about 3.2 percent of a

Table 1.1. Projected Population of the World and Major Areas, 2015, 2030, 2050, and 2100 (in millions)

Major Area	2015	2030	2050	2100
World	7,349	8,501	9,725	11,213
Africa	1,186	1,679	2,478	4,387
Asia	4,393	4,923	5,267	4,889
Europe	738	734	707	646
Latin America and Caribbean	634	721	784	721
North America	358	396	433	500
Oceania	39	47	57	71

Source: United Nations Department of Economic and Social Affairs, Population Division, *World Population Prospects: The 2015 Revision*, 7.

global population of more than seven billion.[34] If all the world's international migrants were to form their own country, a "migration nation" as it were, it would have the fifth-largest population behind only China (1.3 billion), India (1.2 billion), the United States (320 million), and Indonesia (255 million).

Looking ahead to the coming decades and further into the second half of the twenty-first century, we see that most population growth will probably be in developing regions of the Global South. Africa, the world's second-largest continent and home to fifty-five countries, is predicted to grow from an estimated 1.1 billion people in 2015 to an astounding 2.4 billion by 2050.[35] At the same time, the economically developed countries of the Global North are expected to grow only minimally in the coming century. According to the United Nations

Table 1.2. International Migrant Stock by Development Level and Major Area, 1990–2010 (in millions)

	1990	2000	2010
World	154.2	174.5	220.7
Developed Regions	82.3	103.4	129.7
Developing Regions	71.9	71.1	91.0
Africa	15.6	15.6	17.1
Asia	49.9	50.4	67.8
Europe	49.0	56.2	69.2
Latin American and Caribbean	7.1	6.5	8.1
North America	27.8	40.4	51.2
Oceania	4.7	5.4	7.3

Source: United Nations Department of Economic and Social Affairs, Population Division (2013), *International Migration Report 2013*, 1.

Population Division, their populations would in fact decline "were it not for the net increase due to migration from developing to developed countries."[36] Europe is projected to have the least growth and its population is expected to rapidly age and shrink.[37] This is, in fact, already happening.

The extreme nature of the demographic drop-off can be seen in places like the once-heavily populated province of Galicia in northwestern Spain, where every second village has been abandoned and where whole villages have been put up for sale. Maria Benedicta Fernandez, an elderly woman who left her ancestral hamlet and moved to a nearby town with more amenities, summed up the demographic situation in forthright terms: "Everyone else left, too, or they've died, and the local school closed. There aren't enough children anymore."[38] In neighboring Portugal, where the birthrate has hit an all-time low, the situation is no different. "What we are looking at is a decrease in the total population—and in particular, in the working-age population, because the population is also aging," says professor Arlindo Oliveira, adding that "the weight of the older generations on the working age will be very, very high."[39] In the poor rural province of Alentejo the birthrate has dropped by more than half since the 1980s and led some towns to transform schools for children into nursing homes for the elderly.

Thus we have the major pieces of a global migration puzzle. The combination of past demographic trends, current figures, and future projections suggests that international population flows will not only continue, but increase. World population growth concentrated in the Global South and the likely continued expansion of the world-economy point toward more international migration in general, and greater South to North migration in particular. Wealthy countries that are aging and shrinking will need young workers to pay taxes, contribute to the national economy, and care for the elderly. Conveniently, countries in Africa, Asia, and the Middle East will have precisely the labor source that is necessary. Yet despite regional demographic and economic differences that could potentially be solved to everyone's mutual benefit, the developed countries of the Global North are building bigger fences, beefing up security, and implementing restrictive immigration policies. While globalization is eliminating barriers between countries and making it easier for goods and capital to move around the world, many developed countries are concurrently putting up barriers to people and making it hard for them to migrate. Why is this happening, what explains these apparent contradictions, and how can we make sense of the movement of hundreds of millions of people across the planet?

EXPLAINING GLOBAL MIGRATION

Some theorists equate globalization with the expansion of the global economy, which continues to interconnect and transform our world. Others view globalization through a neorealist lens and argue that sovereign nation-states remain the most powerful actors in the global arena. Still others focus on a "world polity" made up of states and international organizations that interact with each other in a global context and are heavily influenced by a relatively homogenous global culture. Then there are those who maintain that a world culture exists that is comprised of many subcultures interacting with each other in complex ways. They argue that global society is characterized by a simultaneous homogeneity and heterogeneity as people and nation-states are compelled to form their own identities in an interdependent world.[40] But where do international migrants fit into these theories?

A century before globalization became a buzzword, the geographer Ernst Georg Ravenstein attempted to systematically examine the process of international migration. Born in 1834 in Frankfurt am Main, Germany, he moved at age eighteen to Great Britain, where he married an Englishwoman, became a citizen, and worked for the British War Office from 1854 to 1872.[41] He is best known today for three erudite articles on "The Laws of Migration" published in *The Geographical Magazine* (1876) and *Journal of the Royal Statistical Society of London* (1885 and 1889). In his 1885 article he noted that "it was a remark of the late Dr. William Farr, to the effect that migration appeared to go on without any definite law" that first directed his attention to the subject.[42] As a result, Ravenstein gathered census data on Great Britain, continental Europe, and North America and set about looking for the root causes and consequences of late nineteenth-century migration.

Much of the scholarship on international migration today rests on the foundational themes mentioned in Ravenstein's "Laws of Migration" and many of his original observations are germane to the twenty-first century. He wrote, for example, that he did "not question for a moment that the principal, though not the only cause of migration, has to be sought for in overpopulation in one part of the country, whilst there exist elsewhere underdeveloped resources which hold out greater promise for remunerative labour."[43] In addition, he noted that "bad or oppressive laws, heavy taxation, an unattractive climate, uncongenial social surroundings, and even compulsion (slave trade, transportation), all have produced and are still producing currents of migration, but none of these currents can compare in volume with that which arises from the desire inherent in most men to 'better' themselves in material prospects."[44] In sum, Ravenstein observed forces that pushed people out of their homelands (e.g., overcrowding, poverty, environmental factors, war) and pulled them into new places (jobs, opportunity, freedom, available land). These forces were later identified as push and pull forces, and came to be known as "push-pull theory."

Modern scholars sometimes view push-pull theories as simplistic and unsophisticated. Nonetheless, they remain fundamental to understanding international migration and will in all likelihood remain a significant part of future analyses. When Everett Lee reexamined "The Laws of Migration" in 1966 he suggested that little progress had been made in theorizing about migration in the century that had passed since Ravenstein made his seminal observations—despite the fact that thousands of studies had been done on the subject.[45] At that time the question was also raised in academic circles whether it was "possible to formulate an explanatory theory general enough to cover the whole process of emigration and immigration."[46] Nearly half a century later, the answer is quite clear that no single theory can explain the whole process of global migration. It is simply too big, complex and multifaceted. As table 1.3 indicates, the disciplines of anthropology, demography, economics, geography, history, law, political science, and sociology have produced not one general explanatory theory but rather a multitude of theories.[47] Each academic discipline looks at the subject from its own angle and through its own lens, asks its own set of research questions, and uses different units of analysis, hypotheses, concepts, and methods of inquiry.

Demographers and economists tend to emphasize rational-choice behavior and the cost-benefit decision-making of migrants and migrant groups, while sociologists and political scientists stress the importance of structures and institutions. Anthropologists and geographers focus

Table 1.3. Migration Theories Across Disciplines

Discipline	Research Question(s)	Levels/Units of Analysis	Dominant Theories	Sample Hypothesis
Anthropology	How does migration effect cultural change and affect ethnic identity?	Micro/individuals, households, groups	Relational or structuralist and transnational	Social networks help maintain cultural difference
Demography	How does migration affect population change?	Macro/populations	Rationalist (borrows heavily from economics)	Migration has a major impact on size, but a small impact on age structure
Economics	What explains the propensity to migrate and its effects?	Micro/individuals	Rationalist: cost-benefit and utility-maximizing behavior	Incorporation varies with the level of human capital of immigrants
Geography	What explains the spatial patterns of migration?	Macro, meso, and micro/ individuals, households, and groups	Relational, structural, and transnational	Incorporation depends on ethnic networks and residential patterns
History	How do we understand the immigrant experience?	Micro/individuals and groups	Eschews theory and hypothesis testing	Not applicable
Law	How does the law influence migration?	Macro and micro/the political and legal system	Institutionalist and rationalist (borrows from all the social sciences)	Rights create incentive structures for migration and incorporation
Political Science	Why do states have difficulty controlling migration?	More macro/political and international systems	Institutionalist and rationalist	States are often captured by pro-immigrant interests
Sociology	What explains incorporation and exclusion?	Macro/ethnic groups and social class	Structuralist or institutionalist	Incorporation varies with social and human capital

Source: Brettell and Hollifield (2008), 4.

on the role social and ethnic networks play in international migration. Legal scholars borrow from all of the social sciences and examine the ways in which laws and rights impact human movement. Historians sometimes eschew explicit theory testing and instead concentrate on the immigrant experience itself—and produce some of the best work on migration of all. American historians John Higham, Oscar Handlin, and Marcus Hansen, for example, bring the subject alive in ways that few scholars in other disciplines can match.[48] At the end of the day, however, most studies of global migration use a combination of theoretical approaches and are either implicitly or explicitly interdisciplinary.

How, then, can we best explain the dual processes of globalization and migration? I believe world-systems theory, an approach that views international migration in relation to the history and structure of the global economic market, provides the most compelling explanation.[49] In a nutshell, the argument is that globalization is associated with the expansion of the capitalist world-economy that emerged in Western Europe in the 1500s. Capitalism is a "system defined by the *endless* accumulation of capital," which spread from its European core and penetrated into peripheral regions in Africa, Asia, and the Americas.[50] The eighteenth- and nineteenth-century Industrial Revolution not only displaced European peasants, who moved from rural to urban areas and then to the New World, it also accelerated the colonial quest for land, natural resources, and new markets abroad. It contributed directly to the Atlantic slave trade, which brought at least twelve million African forced migrants to the Americas.

European imperialism disrupted the lives of the colonized peoples to an enormous degree. Traditional ways of life, making a living, and interacting with others were turned upside down by the newly introduced capitalist economy. Land, for instance, was used in new ways. What had once been communal land farmed by indigenous peoples was consolidated into huge plantations that grew just one crop, such as coffee, sugar, or cotton. Small farmers who could not compete, sell their produce, or make a living off the land had to look for other means of livelihood. Dislocated peasants consequently moved from the countryside to cities to look for work. They also migrated abroad, which was facilitated by cultural ties and transportation lines established between core and peripheral countries—for example, between India and Great

Britain, Indonesia and the Netherlands, the Congo and Belgium. By 1900, the capitalist economic market had expanded around the world. When the colonial period came to an end in the mid-twentieth century, neocolonialism remained in its place.

Today, with the collaboration of compliant governments and local elites in the peripheral countries of the Global South, multinational corporations continue to take advantage of the large number of dislocated, unemployed workers. Seeking profit above all else, they exploit people by paying them the lowest possible wage, flouting regulations and despoiling the environment in the process. Despite passionate arguments by conservative interest groups to curtail immigration, pro-business governments of countries in the Global North are reluctant to stop the flow of migrant workers because doing so would lead to lower profits, labor shortages, economic recession, and objections from multinational corporations. At the same time, the global capitalist economy requires skilled labor, which leads to brain drain in less economically developed countries and brain gain in more economically developed countries. The result is a bifurcated economy whereby the populations of Global Cities such as New York, London, and Tokyo are split between a wealthy elite and a large number of low-wage workers—waitresses, cooks, bus drivers, nannies, gardeners—who struggle to survive in the global economy.[51]

When the working poor demand a living wage, seek a fair distribution of wealth, organize politically, or plot revolution, governments use military force and the vast military industrial complex to protect the global market and the interests of the capitalist class. Yet war inevitably results in humanitarian disasters, displaced populations, and refugee flows—which then lead receiving countries to implement restrictive immigration policies to keep unwanted migrants out. It is not just people—such as the thousands of children orphaned by wars in Iraq and Afghanistan—who suffer from war, but also the earth itself. The combination of rapacious capitalism, gluttonous consumerism, and ruinous wars has brought the environment to a breaking point, where climate change and extreme weather are not only displacing people but also threatening the planet with global ecological collapse.

Skeptics are wont to claim that such talk is alarmist. They point out that projections of future climate-related migration are based on mere speculation and no one knows what the future will hold. In response, I argue environmental destruction poses a serious, long-term threat that is likely to have an increasing impact on global migration. Climate-related migration is used here to refer to the movement of people that "occurs when climatic conditions, weather events, changes in those events and conditions, and/or their physical impacts are among the easily recognizable influences on migration, but they need not be the sole cause of the migration event."[52] In straightforward terms, the main problem is that capitalism and the global environment are on a collision course. If globalization continues on its present path, large swaths of the earth will no longer be habitable and the number of environmental migrants will likely reach into the hundreds of millions. While climate change affects the whole world, the hardest hit places will almost certainly be in areas already suffering from poverty, economic underdevelopment, and collapsing ecosystems—that is to say, the Global South.

NORTH AND SOUTH, CORE AND PERIPHERY

In international relations discourse nation-states are classified in a variety of ways, some of which have changed over time. In the decades after World War II it was common to group them into three main tiers. The First World referred to countries allied with the United States during the Cold War (1945–1991), the Second World to the Soviet Union and its mostly Eastern European allies, and the Third World to the remaining countries not aligned with either the United States or Soviet Union. The term First World is still used, but it now refers to capitalist, wealthy, industrialized states of the Global North, while the phrase Second World gradually lost its meaning after the Soviet Union collapsed in 1991. The term Third World (from the French *Tiers-Monde*) refers to the poor, nonindustrialized countries of the world and was widely used before it gradually started to fall out of favor in the 1990s. A keyword search of the British Library catalogue conducted in 2001 revealed that the number of books written on the Third World hit its peak in the mid-1990s, and then dropped off. Intriguingly, the marked decline in the number of publications on the Third World coincided with the rise in the number of books published on globalization. Historian B. R. Tomlinson found that the first books with globalization in their titles appeared in 1988, and "the first year in which more books were published on globalization than on the Third World was 1996. Between

January 1995 and March 2001 there were 358 titles on globalization, and only 162 on the Third World."[53] This pattern indicates not just a change in terminology, but a conceptual shift of focus toward globalization at the beginning of the twenty-first century.

First World countries are now commonly referred to as economically developed, industrialized, and wealthy. In contrast, Third World countries are variously called less economically developed, developing, nonindustrialized, and simply poor. In world-systems theory the two are viewed as a relational pair in which rich, dominant core countries exploit poor, weak peripheral countries. Historically, Europe comprised the core or center of the world-economy, which later expanded to include major countries such as the United States and Japan. Countries in-between the economically developed core and underdeveloped periphery are part of the semi-periphery. When semi-peripheral countries develop economically and succeed in the world-economy they can move into the core; likewise, if they fail they can also move into the periphery. The essential characteristics of the core-periphery relationship are exploitation and inequality of power and wealth, as core countries have long subjugated peripheral countries by colonizing them, extracting resources, and taking advantage of unequal terms of trade.

Geographically, core countries are located in the Global North, primarily in Europe and North America. Peripheral countries are located in the Global South, primarily in Africa, Asia, Latin America, and the Middle East. If we were to draw lines on a map of the world, two of the main borders delineating the core countries concentrated in the Global North from the peripheral countries in the Global South would be the Rio Grande River separating the United States and Mexico, and the Mediterranean Sea separating the European and African continents. These terms, however, are not without contradictions. Australia and New Zealand, for instance, belong to the Global North even though they are in the southern hemisphere. They nonetheless capture, however awkwardly, the general distinctions between a comparatively affluent Europe and poor Africa, or economically developed North America and less economically developed South America. In the ensuing chapters I regard core countries as synonymous with the Global North and peripheral countries as synonymous with the Global South.

In total, approximately 6 billion of the world's nearly 7.4 billion people live in the Global South. According to the International Orga-

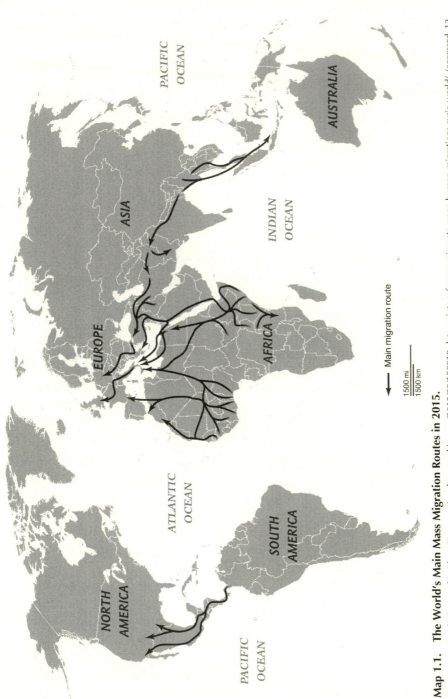

Map 1.1.   The World's Main Mass Migration Routes in 2015.

Sources: National Geographic, http://news.nationalgeographic.com/2015/09/150919-data-points-refugees-migrants-maps-human-migrations-syria-world/ (accessed 12 March 2016); Missing Migrants Project, International Organization for Migration; UNHCR; i-Map; Regional Mixed Migration Secretariat.

nization for Migration (IOM), most international migration originates there as well. An estimated 40 percent goes from the Global South to Global North, 33 percent from South to South, 22 percent from North to North, and 5 percent from North to South. These percentages vary slightly depending on how countries are classified and who makes the calculations. The United Nations Development Programme (UNDP), for instance, reckons that 41 percent of international migration flows from South to North, 41 percent from South to South, 15 percent from North to North, and 3 percent from North to South. Similarly, data from the World Bank indicates that 45 percent flows from South to North, 35 percent South to South, 17 percent North to North, and 3 percent North to South.[54] Final estimates differ somewhat, but the overall pattern remains: most international migrants are from the Global South; the largest flow is South to North and the second largest flow is within the South; relatively few people migrate from rich to poor regions.

CONCLUSION

Globalization is a complex and contested concept. As Anthony Giddens has pointed out, it "is not a single set of processes and does not lead in a single direction. It produces solidarities in some places and destroys them in others. It has quite different consequences on one side of the world from the other. In other words, it is a wholly contradictory process."[55] Indeed, much the same can be said about international migration. Some countries gain hugely by attracting the best and the brightest people while others are underdeveloped by the departure of their talented, young, industrious citizens. Similarly, some individuals benefit enormously from migration; for them globalization means the onset of a borderless world full of promise and opportunity.[56] Others are painfully uprooted and dislocated by war, poverty, and environmental degradation, and fences are built to keep them out.

The forced migration of refugees from the Middle East and North Africa has, for some years now, been among the most prominent issues in world politics. Millions of people like Ali Najaf and his family have fled their war-ravaged homes and thousands have died trying to escape the bloodshed. The ways in which the countries of the Global North have dealt with this mass migration illustrate the tragic contradictions associated with globalization. The wars in Afghanistan, Iraq, Syria,

Libya, and elsewhere are a result of military interventions by the countries of the Global North. In seeking to dominate the Middle East and control the region's natural resources, the governments of the United States and Great Britain, among others, caused a colossal humanitarian disaster. Now they are reluctant to take in people fleeing for their very lives. While barriers to trade, communication, and travel are broken down, these countries are simultaneously enacting policies that protect borders instead of people. The chapters that follow will attempt to make sense of how we arrived at this paradoxical point in history.

CHAPTER 2

HISTORICAL-STRUCTURAL ORIGINS OF GLOBAL MIGRATION

Jan Troell's epic 1971 film *The Emigrants* and its sequel *The New Land* provide some of the starkest visual images of historical migration ever recorded. Set in the mid-nineteenth century, the films portray in vivid pictorial detail the lives of a beleaguered group of Swedes who decide they must leave their home province of Småland in southern Sweden and emigrate to America. The range of factors compelling the main characters to move to Minnesota, which they imagine to be a free and bountiful Promised Land, runs the gamut from economic stress and lack of opportunity to religious persecution and social stigma. Their endearing stories are typical of European peasants migrating to the New World during that time period.

Despite Karl Oskar Nilsson's tremendous work ethic, he and his wife Kristina struggle to eke out a living on a small family farm and can barely feed themselves and their children. Crops fail and their infant daughter dies due to lack of proper food. The barn is burned to the ground after being struck in the middle of the night by a freak bolt of lightning. Their lives are so bleak, luck so bad, and poverty so great that they are irresistibly drawn to the prospect of starting a new life on the other side of the Atlantic Ocean. Kristina, however, has lingering doubts and cautions prophetically that if they leave Sweden, it will be for good, and they will never return or see their hometown, friends, or relatives again.

Robert, Karl Oskar's younger brother, works as an indentured servant on a neighboring farm for a cruel and brutal master who beats him so mercilessly his hearing in one ear is permanently damaged. His half-witted friend, Arvid, works on the farm as well and gets caught up in the dream of moving to the Promised Land. Besides the poverty and abusive working conditions, Arvid also suffers from a false rumor that he once had sexual intercourse with a cow, which gives him all the more reason to want to escape his embarrassing social situation. When Robert reads from a booklet about the United States and says, "even the slaves have a higher standard of living than most European peasants. They are allowed to own their chickens and market the produce themselves," Arvid responds naively, "I'm going to sign on as a slave."[1]

Danjel, a fanatic evangelical preacher who chafes under the strict laws of the Swedish state and Lutheran Church, yearns for more religious freedom. When he tries to preach to a small group of people gathered in his home, the local police arrive and break up the service. Like many other religiously motivated nineteenth-century European migrants, Danjel has megalomaniacal delusions; he believes he has achieved enlightenment, and tells his small flock that God will miraculously grant them the ability to speak English as soon as they arrive on the shores of America. Among his followers is Ulrika, the former town prostitute and social outcast, and her daughter, who also dream of starting anew in a place where their painful pasts no longer haunt them. Lastly, the figure of Jonas Petter is so unhappily married that he is willing to emigrate in order to escape his wife.

The group sets sail for America aboard a cramped wooden ship and must deal with an outbreak of lice, rotten food, and the sudden death in cramped quarters of a fellow passenger. Upon arrival in America they travel by train and steamboat to Minnesota, where they know other Swedes have settled. En route they see enslaved Africans bound together at the neck by thick metal chains, and witness obvious class differences in American society. Robert tries to make sense of the situation and explains to the others that "the way it works here is, those people who have been here long enough are already rich. We're still poor because we just got here. It takes a little time."[2]

As settlers in the New Land of Minnesota, the members of the group embark with varying degrees of success on their new lives as Swedish-Americans. Karl Oskar lays claim to a tract of land, seemingly unaware that he is displacing the local tribe of Indians that lives there. While Karl Oskar is content in America, his continually pregnant wife Kristina never gets over her homesickness for Sweden. Robert and Arvid catch gold rush fever and set off on a disastrous and fatal trip to California. Danjel is able to practice Christianity, in true Protestant fashion, as he sees fit. Ulrika is set free from the toxic shame that dogged her in the Old Country, and she marries an utterly respectable Baptist minister. The saga ends with a final letter home, in which a family friend sends news back to relatives in Småland of Karl Oskar's death.

When Roger Ebert reviewed the film in 1973 he wrote "'The Emigrants' is a special film in that it's Swedish and yet somehow American—in the sense that it tells the story of what America meant for so many millions. When it was over the other evening, the audience applauded; that's a rare thing for a Chicago audience to do, but then 'The Emigrants' is a very rare film."[3] Indeed, by recreating what the migration experience must have been like and bringing to life the voyage and all of its hardships, it offers a powerful and historically accurate glimpse into nineteenth-century trans-Atlantic European migration. What is more, Troell's films, which are based on the books written by Swedish author Vilhelm Moberg, show the origins of Americans of Scandinavian descent who now inhabit much of the upper Midwest of the United States.[4] We see where the blue eyes and blond hair, Protestant work ethic, Nordic social sensibilities, and cultural characteristics of so many present-day Minnesotans originated.[5]

WE ARE ALL IMMIGRANTS

Historical shortsightedness sometimes leads people to think that their ethnic group always inhabited a certain place. In reality, everyone has an ancestor who at one time or another migrated. You just have to go far enough back into history to find that person. When human movement is traced back through time it becomes apparent that Native American Indians, for instance, are descendants of people who travelled over the land bridge between Asia and North America some 15,000 years ago. Asians have distant ancestors who migrated out of the Middle East and North Africa, and Africans experienced thousands of years of mixing of tribes across the continent. To those who are aware of this history and prehistory, it is obvious that humanity is the product of many millennia of migration and intermingling.

We need not dwell on the ancient past or get lost in the slipstream of time, but it is useful to have a basic knowledge of the historical record in order to fully grasp the current state of global migration. Knowledge of the past affects our understanding of the present, which in turn helps us interpret events as they unfold. It shapes our perception of reality and the status quo. It widens our view of politics, deepens our comprehension of complex social issues, and provides a greater awareness of international relations. But where do we start, and how far back into history do we need to look? Unconventional as it may sound, it behooves the educated reader to take a radically universal view and, at the risk of venturing into the fields of astronomy and earth science, roll back the clock as far as possible.

Scientists believe the Big Bang occurred 13.8 billion years ago, and planet earth formed about 4.6 billion years ago. Life on earth appeared in its most basic form at least 3.4 billion years ago, and the supercontinent known as Pangaea started to break apart around 200 million years ago. The dinosaurs ruled the earth for 135 million years until, 65 million years ago, a major asteroid smashed into our blue planet and wiped most of them out (happily, the birds survived). The first ape-like species emerged 15 million years ago and *Homo erectus* (Latin for "upright man") migrated out of Africa over a million years ago. Modern *Homo sapiens* ("wise man") left Africa at least 60,000 years ago and crossed the land bridge between Asia and North America 15,000 years ago before migrating down to the southern tip of South America. Agriculture emerged about 10,000 years ago and writing was invented in ancient Sumer (present-day Iraq) in 3200 BCE. Confucius wrote "do not impose on others what you do not wish for yourself" in the fifth century BCE and Plato wrote his masterpiece *The Republic* in 380 BCE. The Vikings reached Newfoundland in 1000 CE, Gutenberg used a movable-type printing press to print the Bible in 1455, and Neil

Armstrong landed on the moon in 1969. The first book with the word "globalization" in its title was published in 1988.

Looking at the universe across such an expansive time period provides a unique perspective from which to observe twenty-first-century human activity. We see that, in the big picture, the lifespan of any single person is very, very short. We see that it may also be likely humans will go extinct over the next hundred million years or so, just as the dinosaurs and the dodo bird and more than 99 percent of the species that have ever lived on earth have done. Yet we also see, on a less ominous note, that *Homo sapiens* are by nature extremely mobile and adaptable, and have inhabited virtually every part of the globe from the equator to the polar regions. It becomes clear that movement—like birth and death—is part and parcel of the human experience. People have been moving for thousands of years from place to place, region to region, and continent to continent, hindered only by natural geographical barriers, dangerous animals, inhospitable weather, competing tribes, and the like. Migration is natural, necessary for survival, and even a result of our genetic makeup. Ultimately, we see that creating territorial borders and trying to control who crosses them is a relatively recent development in world history.

With this in mind, let us turn to those major historical events that deepen our understanding of the dual processes of globalization and migration. This will shed more light on the historical-structural reasons why, for example, tens of millions of Europeans and Africans crossed the Atlantic and began new lives in the Americas. The explorations of the Vikings—the ancestors of the Swedes portrayed in *The Emigrants*—provide a suitable starting point for our examination of history, for their early arrival in North America signaled the beginning of an extended period of European expansion and conquest. The Vikings were "premodern" seafarers who went boldly into the frigid, unknown waters of the North Atlantic five centuries before their Spanish successors reached the Americas. Christopher Columbus's arrival in the New World coincided with what historians call the beginning of the "modern era" in Europe and the onset of the process we now call globalization.

THE QUEST FOR MATERIAL BENEFITS AND PROFIT

Eric the Red founded the first Viking settlement in Greenland in the year 985. According to legend, his son, Leif Ericson, sailed in the year 1000 to what is now the Canadian province of Newfoundland and

Labrador and is credited by some as the first European to reach North America.[6] The story of this discovery is recorded in *The Saga of Eric the Red*, which describes how Leif met with Norwegian King Olaf Tryggvason, who asked whether it was his purpose to return to Greenland in the summer. When Leif said it was, the King approved and responded, "thither thou shalt go upon my errand, to proclaim Christianity there."[7] On his voyage home, however, Leif was blown off course and landed not in Greenland, but Newfoundland: "For a long time he was tossed about upon the ocean, and came upon lands of which he had previously had no knowledge. There were self-sown wheat fields and vines growing there. There were also those trees there which are called 'mausur' [maple], and of all these they took specimens."[8] This saga provides one of the earliest written accounts of North America, which (perhaps because of the aforementioned grape vines) the Vikings called Vinland the Good.

Leif was consequently given the nickname "Leif the Lucky" for his noble goodness and for furthering the Christian cause. The Scandinavian settlement in North America, however, was not so lucky. For reasons that are not entirely clear, the Vikings in Vinland disappeared. Belligerent as they were, they most likely came into conflict with the native peoples of the area and, failing to adapt fully to their surroundings, either died out or abandoned the place. The remains of their settlement—old-Norse style buildings and artifacts such as a forge, furnace, and small iron objects—were found in 1960 near L'Anse aux Meadows at the tip of Newfoundland's Great Northern Peninsula.[9] The fascinating thing about the Viking exploration of North America is that there is, in fact, a written record, albeit one that mixes fact and fantasy. There was for some time uncertainty about whether Leif Ericson actually made it to Newfoundland, but these doubts were quelled when the Norse settlement in Canada was excavated.

By the fifteenth century, innovations in shipbuilding, printing, mapping, and navigation allowed European explorers to sail to nearly every corner of the globe. Bartolomeu Dias led an expedition from Portugal down the length of the African coast and was the first European to round the southern tip of the African continent in February 1488. The trip was successful in part because he sailed with three ships, one of which stopped along the way in present-day Angola and waited with extra supplies for the others to return. When Dias rounded the southern tip of Africa, he called it Cape of Storms, which was later renamed Cape of Good Hope by Portuguese King Manuel I because it had a less dangerous, more promising ring to it. A decade later, Portuguese navigator Vasco da Gama sailed around the southern tip of Africa to India and back, thereby establishing the lucrative and long-hoped-for sea route linking Europe and South Asia. The so-called Age of Discovery had begun.

When Italian-born Christopher Columbus landed on the Island of San Salvador on October 12, 1492, mistakenly thinking he had reached India and thus naming the native inhabitants "Indians," his intentions were clear. We know because he spelled them out in his own words in written reports to Ferdinand and Isabella, the King and Queen of Spain. He wrote that the islands he discovered (now the Bahamas, Cuba, and Haiti) on the first of his four voyages to the Americas were full of gold and natural resources. He described the native inhabitants as being "so free with all they possess, that no one would believe it without having seen it. Of anything they have, if you ask them for it, they never say no; rather they invite the person to share it, and show as much love as if they were giving their hearts."[10] He promised to deliver as much gold, spices, cotton, aloe wood, and as many Indian slaves as the King and Queen desired. He concluded that "Christendom ought to feel joyful and make celebrations and give solemn thanks to the Holy Trinity with many solemn prayers for the great exaltation which it will have, in the turning of so many peoples to our holy faith, and afterwards for material benefits, since not only Spain but all Christians will hence have refreshment and profit."[11] Columbus's letters are remarkable in many ways, but particularly because they candidly reveal the European desire for gold and slaves in the name of Christianity.

The quest for natural resources and profit and the introduction of a powerful new religion led to massive disruption everywhere the Europeans went. The impact was enormous, and life in those places—all of the Americas, Africa, and Asia—would never be the same. To get an idea of the scale of the intrusion and amount of violence associated with it, consider what was known as *El Requerimiento* (The Requirement), a document read by conquistadors in Spanish to the native inhabitants as soon as they disembarked from their ships. Obviously incomprehensible to the peoples it was meant to reach, it included the following: "I implore you to recognize the Church as a lady and in the name of the Pope take the King as lord of this land and obey his mandates. If you do not do it, I tell you that with the help of God I will enter powerfully against you all. I will make war everywhere and every way that I can."[12] For good measure, it concluded by shifting blame for the coming onslaught onto the hapless victims: "I will subject you to the yoke and obedience to the Church and to his majesty. I will take your women and children and make them slaves. . . . The deaths and injuries that you will receive from here on will be your own fault and not that of his majesty nor of the gentleman that accompany me."[13] Bizarre as it sounds to modern ears, reading The Requirement aloud likely gave the conquistadors a psychological sense of absolution before they began their ruthless campaign of subjugation.

Europeans and Native Americans saw each other in radically different ways. Columbus reported the Indians "believe very firmly that I, with these ships and people, came from the sky, and in this belief they everywhere received me . . . with loud cries of, 'Come, Come! See the people from the sky!'"[14] European explorers, in contrast, typically regarded the natives as savages. As Alfred Crosby writes in *The Columbian Exchange: Biological and Cultural Consequences of 1492*, most Spaniards hardly knew what to make of the Indians they encountered and assumed, in the end, that they were "in league with Hell" and "allies of the Devil."[15] This way of thinking—of condemning, projecting, and othering—provides insight into the European mind at the time and helps to understand the colonization that followed.

When the Europeans arrived in the *Mundus Novus*, as they called it, they brought with them things that had not previously been there and likewise returned with items that revolutionized the Old World. They brought sugar and coffee, for example, which was well suited to growing in the Americas and would soon be cultivated on massive plantations. They introduced crops such as wheat and barley, and animals such as horses and cows. When they emptied the ballast out of their ships they unwittingly introduced the earthworm to the Americas (it had died out in the last ice age), which began a continent-wide ecological transformation. Without realizing it, they imported a bevy of diseases including smallpox (which the Indians called Rotting Face), measles, typhus, and cholera that would eventually kill an estimated 90 percent of the native inhabitants of the Americas.[16] In other words, "before Europeans initiated the Columbian Exchange of germs and viruses, the peoples of the Americas suffered no smallpox, no measles, no chickenpox, no influenza, no typhus, no typhoid or parathyroid fever, no diphtheria, no cholera, no bubonic plague, no scarlet fever, no whooping cough, and no malaria."[17] Native Americans had never experienced these diseases, as the Europeans had, and thus succumbed in huge numbers.

Why had Europeans already been exposed to such ghastly viruses, and how did they so quickly conquer the Americas? The answer has much to do with geography and environmental circumstances. As Jared Diamond explains in *Guns, Germs and Steel: The Fates of Human Societies*, "different rates of development on different continents, from 11,000 B.C. to A.D. 1500, were what led to the technological and political inequalities of 1500."[18] The emergence of agriculture, metallurgy, and writing, for instance, occurred earlier in Europe than North America. In addition, Europeans had lived for thousands of years in close proximity to domesticated animals, such as cows, horses, pigs, and sheep, which led to exposure to germs and increased resistance to such diseases as smallpox and measles. Native Americans did not have as many domesticated animals, were not exposed to the germs that accompanied them, and thus had little natural resistance.

Europeans took many things home with them, as well, including the scourge of venereal syphilis. While it is hard to tell precisely how it happened five centuries ago, the most plausible hypothesis is that Columbus's men, eighty-eight in total, disembarked from the *Santa Maria*, the *Nina*, and the *Pinta* (a Spanish nickname for "prostitute") and had sexual intercourse with the Native American women. When they returned to Spain they carried syphilis with them and, probably after passing it on to port city prostitutes, unleashed the fearsome disease upon the continent. It spread unchecked and reached epidemic proportions within only a few short years. European countries took turns blaming each other, as the French called it the "Italian Disease," the Germans called it the "French Disease," and the Russians called it the "Polish Disease." Syphilis today is cured simply with penicillin, but in the sixteenth century there was little that could be done. One supposed remedy was mercury, a toxic chemical, but that was as likely to harm the patient as ameliorate the dreadful symptoms. Otherwise, there was no cure and patients were left to endure painful and stigmatizing body lesions, boils, rotting flesh, and ultimately dementia and madness.

Mercifully, Europeans returned from the Americas with more than just pestilence. They brought previously unknown plants and foods that would profoundly transform society. Some of the most notable were potatoes (and sweet potatoes), tomatoes, corn (also called maize), green peppers, eggplants, cacao beans, and tobacco. The potato quickly became not only an important part of the European diet but also intertwined with the course of European history. The humble potato helped the Irish population grow to eight million in 1845, but then an airborne fungus turned the leaves of potato plants black and caused the tuber to rot. When the Potato Famine struck between 1845 and 1852, one million Irish died and another million emigrated. The Dutch, Germans, and French called the potato an "earth apple" (*aardappel, Erdapfel* and *pomme de terre*) and, along with much of the rest of Europe, made it a staple of their daily meals. The Italians used the tomato to liven up their pizza and pasta, so that today it is hard to imagine Mediterranean cuisine without it. Tobacco, of course, made lifelong addicts of millions people around the world and became one of the most valuable cash crops of all time.

The Columbian Exchange of food, viruses, and ideas led to population growth in Europe and a precipitous decline in the Americas. It has never been clear exactly what the total population of the Americas was before Columbus's arrival—it persists as one of history's great debates—but one estimate puts it in the year 1492 at 53.9 million (3.8 in North America, 17.2 in Mexico, 5.6 in Central America, 3.0 in the Caribbean, and 24.3 in South America).[19] Quite obvious, though, is the abrupt crash that followed the European arrival: by 1650 the total population of the Americas had dropped to an estimated 5.6 million, a decline of almost 90 percent in just over 150 years.[20] In contrast, the population of Europe grew rapidly during this same time period, in part due to the arrival and cultivation of new calorie-rich foods from the Americas. In 1500 there were 156 European cities with more than 10,000 inhabitants and only four with more than 100,000 (Paris, Milan, Venice, and Naples), but by 1800 there were 363 cities with 10,000 and seventeen larger than 100,000.[21]

Population growth in Europe coincided with the emergence of the Industrial Revolution in the eighteenth century. European peasants dislocated by this economic transformation understandably started looking abroad as a way to escape their dire economic and social circumstances. The exodus out of Europe to the Americas, Australia, New Zealand, South Africa, and European colonies abroad turned into the largest transoceanic migration in human history. The second largest was the involuntary migration of African slaves to the Americas. Let us turn first to migration out of Europe.

TRANS-ATLANTIC EUROPEAN MIGRATION

Fundamental social, political, and economic changes associated with the Industrial Revolution resulted in large-scale internal and international migration. Economic historian Karl Polanyi called the enormous shift from rural agrarianism to urban industrialism "the Great Transformation" and pointed out that the new tools of production led to a "catastrophic dislocation of the lives of the common people."[22] If we examine England as a case study in the years leading up to the Industrial Revolution, we see clearly the origins of this dislocation.

For centuries England had an "open-field" system of agriculture that set aside land for communal use.[23] The open fields were divided into narrow strips and farmed by members of the community. The system was antiquated and inefficient and did not always yield enough food because much of the arable land was left fallow. If the weather was bad, it negatively affected the harvest and people went hungry. An agricultural revolution in the late seventeenth century changed all this. It introduced the idea of enclosing and consolidating the previously open fields, so one person rather than the community owned the land. Private ownership inspired innovation in farming, such as rotating crops—wheat-turnips-barley-clover—so that more fallow land could be used. Consequently, the fenced-in land was more intensively farmed and more food for people and fodder for animals was produced. New farming methods and crops such as the potato led to less famine and provided paid work for people on the enclosed farms, but it also meant the disappearance of what had previously been common land and the displacement of the people who had traditionally farmed it. As Oscar Handlin notes in *The Uprooted*, the peasant's "loss of the land was a total calamity. The land was not an isolated thing in his life. It was a part of the family and of the village, a pivot of a complex circle of relationships, the primary index of his own, his family's status. What was a man without land?"[24]

As the old feudal system evolved into a more productive and (for the landowner) profitable capitalist way of farming, the population was affected in other important ways as well. By the end of the seventeenth century bubonic plague was brought under control by quarantining port cities, isolating the sick so as not to infect others, and reducing the population of flea-carrying rats. The Black Death had for three centuries slowed population growth—the 1665 London plague, for instance, killed almost 20 percent of the city's population—but when this check was lifted the population exploded in the eighteenth century.[25] The combination of more food, less famine, and the disappearance of the plague was a great achievement, but with fewer people dying of starvation and disease the population grew quickly. As industry expanded, peasants from the countryside moved to urban areas to work in the textile mills. This shift was seen clearly in the West Riding of Yorkshire in northern England, where the population almost doubled from 564,000 in 1801 to 980,000 in 1831.[26] The number of English living in towns of 5,000 or more inhabitants rose from 8.3 percent in 1600 to 40 percent in 1850.[27] Emigration to North America and the colonies provided an outlet for this population pressure.

One of the eighteenth century's most important technical advancements was the invention of the steam engine. In 1760 James Watt produced an efficient coal-fired steam engine that was soon put to a wide variety of uses. In particular, it revolutionized the cotton industry as power-looms began to mass-produce cotton cloth. Steam was used to power boats and locomotives as well. The first steam-powered train appeared in 1825 and ushered in a boom in railroad building across not only England but also elsewhere in Europe, North America, and around the world. The growth and expansion of the railroads lowered transportation costs of finished goods and increased the size of the economic market. The British government helped in the effort to build and finance the railroads, roads, and canals used to transport goods and people across the country and overseas. The crux of the matter here is that when migrants moved abroad they traveled on ships that were part of the transportation network interconnecting the rapidly expanding world-economy.

Behind these revolutions in agriculture, industry, energy, and transportation was a prevailing belief among the political elites in mercantilism. This economic philosophy lasted from the sixteenth to the eighteenth centuries and dictated that the government should regulate trade and commerce with the goal of increasing state power, wealth, and security. The means to these ends included favoring exports over imports, turning raw materials from the colonies into finished goods, and selling as many manufactured products to as many people as possible. Mercantilism gradually morphed into capitalism, the closely related system in which trade, commerce, and industry are allowed to run their course unfettered by government intervention. Adam Smith famously described it in *The Wealth of Nations* (1776) as allowing the "invisible hand" of the market to guide the economy.[28] He went on to sum up the capitalist mentality this way: "It is not from the benevolence of the butcher, the brewer, or the baker that we expect our dinner, but from their regard of their own interest. We address ourselves not to their humanity, but to their self-love, and never talk to them of our own necessities, but of their advantages."[29] The right to own private property and maximize profits, often by making employees work harder, faster, and longer, was accepted as part of the natural order of life. However, as illustrated in nineteenth-century England, the problem with the endless pursuit of profit and unabashed self-interest is that it easily mutates into greed and exploitation.

In *The Condition of the Working Class in England* (1844) Friedrich Engels described the truly wretched plight of the working poor. He saw in the slums of England's cities a brutal mix of poverty, sickness, and pollution. He came across working-class neighborhoods where the streets were "generally unpaved, rough, dirty, filled with vegetable and animal refuse, without sewers or gutters, but supplied with foul, stagnant, pools instead."[30] He found Irish immigrants among the poorest of the poor, "sinking daily deeper, losing daily more and more of their power to resist the demoralizing influence of want, filth, and evil surroundings."[31] He witnessed whole families living in single barren rooms, sleeping together in a heap, with boards pulled up in the floor serving as a toilet hole. In sum, he documented how a small number of people were getting rich off the labor of the masses, who were overworked, underpaid, and living in squalor.

Safety regulations, minimum wages, and child labor laws did not exist at the height of the Industrial Revolution. Gruesome injuries occurred in the factories as people got fingers, hands, arms, and other limbs lopped off or mangled in the machinery. There is no way to overstate the depravity of life in the factories. They were a living hell, as shown in the following interview conducted in 1832 between House of Commons representative Michael Sadler and twenty-two-year-old former child laborer Mathew Crabtree:

> Have you ever been employed in a factory?—Yes.
> At what age did you first go to work in one?—Eight.
> How long did you continue in that occupation?—Four years.
> Will you state the hours of labour at the period when you first went to the factory, in ordinary times?—From 6 in the morning to 8 at night.
> Fourteen hours?—Yes.
> With what intervals for refreshment and rest?—An hour at noon.
> Then you had no resting time allowed in which to take your breakfast, or what is in Yorkshire called your "drinking"?—No.
> When trade was brisk what were your hours?—From 5 in the morning to 9 in the evening.
> Sixteen hours?—Yes.
> With what intervals at dinner?—An hour.
> How far did you live from the mill?—About two miles.
> Was there any time allowed for you to get your breakfast in the mill?—No.
> Did you take it before you left your home?—Generally.
> During those long hours of labour could you be punctual; how did you awake?—I seldom did awake spontaneously; I was most generally awoke or lifted out of bed, sometimes asleep, by my parents.
> Were you always in time?—No.
> What was the consequence if you had been too late?—I was most commonly beaten.
> Severely?—Very severely, I thought.[32]

Crabtree went on to explain in candid terms how the nonstop factory work and beatings left him tired, sick, injured, physically stunted, mentally anxious, and exceedingly unhappy. He was not alone. Millions of other people were caught in these factories that came to be known as "Satanic Mills." It is no wonder European peasants working in such unforgiving conditions felt alienated and estranged from their labor, from themselves, from their lives, and wanted to escape.[33] The prospect of moving to the New World offered a way out, and the idea that a person or family could start anew and actually own a plot of land was immensely powerful.

My own ancestors, in fact, emigrated from northern England at the peak of the Industrial Revolution. According to a brief family history book, Henry Dickinson, Sr., left the West Riding of Yorkshire in September 1830 with his two eldest sons, William and Henry, and set sail for the United States. Leaving behind exploitive working conditions, poverty, overcrowding, and hard times, they arrived after seven weeks and five days in Philadelphia where they established themselves and began working. Henry Sr. then returned to England to get his wife Diana and remaining six children before moving the entire clan to Morgan County, Ohio, where he lived out the remainder of his life. Henry Jr. continued migrating westward to the state of Indiana (literally "Land of the Indians"), where he found "Indian trails and dancing floors and Indian gardens and burial grounds, Indian ponies and Indian life."[34] Reflecting typical Anglo-American attitudes of the early twentieth century, the family history book concludes that "all our manufacturing pursuits, all the material results of school and church work, all this civilization and prosperity attained since the moccasined Indian ceased here to tread" was done in the spirit of progress.[35]

The experience of the Dickinson family fits a common pattern of nineteenth-century migration to the United States. The patriarch and two eldest sons migrated first to get the lay of the land in a major eastern port city, then were joined by the rest of the family. They soon moved west and, instead of being troubled by the displacement of the Native Americans, felt it was right and good to bring European civilization to the American frontier. They were eager to turn what they saw as barren, unused land into farms, orchards, pastures, towns, and villages. Like many other settlers of the upper Midwest of the United States they were churchgoing Methodists and abolitionists. Being White Anglo-Saxon Protestants, they also enjoyed the enormous privileges that came along with being members of the dominant race and class, language and religion. They found work, farmed the land, and thrived in their new environment.

Similar to Karl Oskar Nilsson and the group of Swedes portrayed in *The Emigrants*, the Dickinsons were part of the massive nineteenth-century migration that commenced in the 1830s. In the words of the great immigration historian Marcus Lee Hansen, migrants of that period who settled America came largely "from Ireland, the Highlands of Scotland and the mountains of Wales—regions where the language and blood were predominantly Celtic and where the land system grew directly out of the agrarian customs of the early tribes."[36] In the decades that followed, tens of millions of Europeans emigrated, many of whom were escaping miserable social conditions brought on by unfettered industrialization. Representing a kind of modern-day Promised Land, America gave them the chance to go confidently in the direction of their dreams, as Henry David Thoreau said, and live the life they had imagined for themselves.

AN AMERICAN EMPIRE

Adam Smith had good reason to believe "the discovery of America and that of a passage to the East Indies by the Cape of Good Hope, are the two greatest and most important events recorded in the history of mankind."[37] They were great because, from a political economist's perspective, the penetration of capitalism into Asia combined with the European conquest of the North American continent led to a massive expansion of the capitalist world-economy. At the same time, from a migration historian's perspective, the New World provided an outlet for millions of European immigrants. The United States, in particular, mixed capitalism and migration into the fiber of its national being from the very beginning. One of the stated reasons for breaking away from Great Britain was that the British interfered with the free movement of the early settlers. The 1776 Declaration of Independence complains that King George III "endeavored to prevent the population of these States; for that purpose, obstructing the laws for naturalization of foreigners, refusing to pass others to encourage their migration hither, and raising the conditions of new appropriations of lands."[38] The migration flow could not be held back, though, and those who could reach America's shores were allowed to stay. With the exception of exclusionary laws against Chinese immigrants, known criminals, and prostitutes, there were relatively few restrictions to entry (compared to today), no officials to check entry documents, and no national immigration offices prior to the 1880s.

As the late migration scholar Aristide Zolberg argued in *A Nation by Design: Immigration Policy in the Fashioning of America*, nineteenth-century U.S. immigration policy "involved from the outset a combination of disparate elements designed to facilitate or even stimulate the entry of immigrants deemed valuable while deterring those considered undesirable, and occasionally even going beyond this to rid the nation of populations already in its midst."[39] In other words, for much of American history the metaphorical gates to the country were wide open for most Europeans. Those who could get to America were let in, largely because there was no real way to keep them out, while Native Americans were put on reservations or actively killed off and Africans were kept in slavery and even encouraged to remigrate. The underlying sentiment in favor of openness was articulated by Herman Melville, the celebrated author of *Moby-Dick*, who himself had seen firsthand the sheer hunger behind mass emigration from Ireland. "Let us waive that agitated national topic, as to whether such multitudes of foreign poor should be landed on our American shores; let us waive it, with the only thought that if they can get here, they have God's right to come; though they bring all Ireland and her miseries with them. For the whole world is the patrimony of the whole world."[40]

The United States inspired a great deal of optimism among European immigrants who had left behind poverty and overcrowding. Newspaper editor John O'Sullivan articulated the hopefulness associated with the United States in an 1839 essay entitled "The Great Nation of Futurity," in which he wrote "the far-reaching, the boundless future will be the era of American greatness. In its magnificent domain of space and time, the nation of many nations is destined to manifest to mankind the excellence of divine principles."[41] From here the idea of Manifest Destiny—that is, that God had ordained that America should stretch from the Atlantic to Pacific coasts—entered the American vocabulary.

By the mid-nineteenth century the United States did indeed stretch from coast to coast, but the expansion and migration of people across North America was not without its glaring contradictions. Europeans fleeing oppression and misery in the Old World turned around and oppressed Africans and Indians in the New World. They also came into conflict with Spanish-speaking Mexicans in the American Southwest. In Texas, for example, white residents did not hesitate to expel Mexicans living there, as indicated in the following newspaper excerpt cited in Frederick Olmsted's 1859 *A Journey Through Texas*:

> The people of Matagorda county have held a meeting and ordered every Mexican to leave the county. To strangers this may seem wrong, but we hold it to be perfectly right and highly necessary; but a word of explanation should be given. In the first place, then, there are none but the lower class or "Peon" Mexicans in the county; secondly, they have no fixed domicile, but hang around the plantations, taking the likeliest negro girls for wives; and, thirdly, they often steal horses, and these girls, too, and endeavor to run them to Mexico. We should rather have anticipated an appeal to Lynch law, than the mild course which has been adopted.[42]

Such quotes—plainly referring to Peon Mexicans, plantations, negro girls, and lynching—shed light on the realities of America's westward expansion.

There was no shortage of Americans who embraced imperialism. Albert J. Beveridge, Republican senator from Indiana (1899–1911), argued for both an American empire and the expansion of the global market. He claimed in 1900 that the Philippines should be "ours forever, 'territory belonging to the United States,' as the Constitution calls them. And just beyond the Philippines are China's illimitable markets. We will not retreat from either. We will not repudiate our duty in the archipelago. We will not abandon our opportunity in the Orient."[43] He went on to articulate the broader goal: "Our largest trade henceforth must be with Asia. The Pacific Ocean is our ocean. More and more Europe will manufacture the most it needs, secure from its colonies the most it consumes. Where shall we turn for consumers of our surplus?"[44] According to Beveridge the answer lay in China, whose massive market promised a huge number of consumers to whom American businessmen could one day sell products.

Beveridge's line of thinking conveyed the logic of capitalism in remarkably pure form—expand the economic market, exploit people and natural resources, and pursue profit above all else. It would seem to exemplify the famous nineteenth-century observation that "the need of a constantly expanding market for its products chases the bourgeoisie over the whole surface of the globe. It must nestle everywhere, settle everywhere, establish connexions everywhere."[45] Over the course of the twentieth century this expansion would, in practice, lead to deadly conflicts such as the Vietnam and Iraq Wars, which killed millions of people. But before we get to neocolonialism and the modern language of economic globalization—privatization, deregulation, trade liberalization, tax cuts, and austerity measures—let us return to the corollary of European transoceanic migration, namely the forced migration of Africans to the Americas.

SLAVERY

European and African migrations to the New World provide a study in marked contrasts. While Europeans fled grinding poverty, economic exploitation, and an untold number of hardships, the African experience was different in that it was indescribably violent and outright deadly. The forced migration of an estimated twelve million African slaves to the Americas between the sixteenth and nineteenth centuries was marked by a vast amount of dehumanization, cruelty, racism, and murder. Not only did it profoundly affect the course of history in both Africa and the Americas, it signaled a dark, new, unprecedented era of globalization.

As indicated in table 2.1, the number of African immigrants arriving in North America, the Caribbean, Spanish America, and Brazil increased steadily over several centuries. Prior to 1600, some 125,000 slaves were brought to the New World, compared to 1.5 million in the seventeenth century, and six million in the eighteenth. Institutionalized slavery gradually came to an end in the nineteenth century, as Great Britain ended the slave trade in 1807 and the practice of slavery in 1833. The United States made importing slaves illegal in 1808 and, after fighting a bloody civil war, abolished it for good in 1865. Yet it lasted until 1886 in Cuba and 1888 in Brazil, by which time millions of Africans had been forcibly brought to the Americas.

How could such an evil thing as the slave trade occur? One of the driving forces behind the bondage and trade of humans as a commodity was the insatiable need for labor in the New World. Indians did not make good slaves, because they died under the harsh conditions of forced labor or simply ran away. Indentured servants were an option, but they were more expensive and expected to earn their freedom after a period of servitude. That left Africans, who were made to work

Table 2.1. African Immigrants, by Period and Place of Arrival (All Figures in Thousands of Persons)

Region	To 1600	1600–1640	1640–1700	1700–1760	1760–1800
North America (British, French, Spanish)	—	1	20	171	177
Caribbean—non-Spanish	—	9	454	1623	1,809
British Caribbean	—	8	255	900	1,085
French Caribbean	—	1	155	474	573
Other Caribbean	—	—	44	249	151
Spanish America	75	269	186	271	235
Spanish Caribbean	7	20	14	27	140
Mexico and Central America	23	70	48	13	5
Venezuela—Columbia—Peru	45	135	93	160	60
La Plata—Bolivia	—	44	30	71	30
Brazil	50	160	400	960	726
Total	125	439	1,060	3,025	2,947

Source: Manning (1993), 280.

for free and were enslaved for life. Besides the need for labor, the slave trade was driven by racism, greed, and the tremendous profits derived from the infamous Triangular Trade between Europe, Africa, and the Americas. In this global business scheme, ships left Europe loaded with manufactured goods such as cloth, guns, iron, and beer, and sailed to West Africa, where the products were traded and exchanged for slaves. They then sailed across the Atlantic to the West Indies and North America, sold the slaves, and took on goods such as sugar, tobacco, lumber, furs, rice, cotton, and rum before returning to Europe. The navigation route interconnected the continents on both sides of the Atlantic, so that in reality it was more than just triangular. It flowed in many conceivable ways, but generally included stops in Europe (e.g., Britain, France, Holland, Spain), Africa (the so-called Ivory, Gold, and Slave Coasts), and the Americas (the United States, Brazil, Haiti, Jamaica, Cuba).

The process of forced migration involved multiple stages, usually beginning with capture in Africa and transportation to a coastal port. The largest number of slaves came from West and West Central Africa, especially the Bights of Benin and Biafra—the bays on either side of the Niger Delta, stretching from Ghana, Togo, and Benin to Nigeria, Cameroon, Equatorial Guinea, and Gabon. African tribes collaborated in the process and would often capture their victims in war and sell or barter them to white traders for such things as guns and liquor. The following story recounted in *A Narrative of the Life and Adventures of Charles Bell, A Black Man* (1854), is representative of an African being captured and, as the saying goes, "sold down the river":

> The village was surrounded by enemies, who attacked us with clubs, long wooden spears, and bows and arrows. After fighting for more than an hour, those who were not fortunate enough to run away were made prisoners. It was not the object of our enemies to kill; they wished to take us alive and sell us as slaves. I was knocked down by a heavy blow of a club, and when I recovered from the stupor that followed, I found myself tied fast. . . . We were immediately led away from this village, through the forest, and were compelled to travel all day as fast as we could walk. . . . We came in sight of what appeared to me the most wonderful object in the world; this was a large ship at anchor in the river. When our raft came near the ship, the white people—for such they were on board—assisted to take us on the deck. . . . I had never

seen white people before and they appeared to me the ugliest creatures in the world. The persons who brought us down the river received payment for us [from] the people in the ship, in various articles, of which I remember that a keg of liquor, and some yards of blue and red cotton cloth were the principal.[46]

Slaves were then crammed into ships for the ten-week voyage across the Atlantic Ocean, called the Middle Passage because it was usually the second leg of the Triangular Trade route. Slave trader Thomas Philip wrote in 1693 that captured Africans had such fear of being shipped across the Atlantic they would jump overboard into shark-infested waters rather than endure the journey. The sharks, anticipating both live and dead bodies being thrown into the sea, followed the ships out of port and into the Atlantic. After buying 480 male and 220 female slaves (a typical ratio), Philip sailed from the West African island of São Tomé to the Caribbean island of Barbados in two months and eleven days. "We often at sea, in the evenings, would let the slaves come up into the sun to air themselves," he wrote, "and make them jump and dance for an hour or two to our bagpipes, harp, and fiddle, by which exercise to preserve them in health."[47] Despite his efforts, fourteen of his crew and 320 slaves became sick and died of severe dysentery. "By their mortality our voyages are ruin'd," he complained of his slaves' deaths, "and we pine and fret ourselves to death, to think that we should undergo such misery, and take so much pains to so little purpose."[48] For Philip the misery was financial, because he got paid only for slaves delivered to Barbados alive.

The majority of slaves were taken to British and French colonies in the Caribbean or to Brazil. Smaller numbers were brought to North and Central America, the Spanish Caribbean, Peru, and Argentina. They were sold on the auction block and taken to the place of forced labor where they worked on sugar, cotton, tobacco, and coffee plantations, in mines, and as domestic servants. In the mid-nineteenth-century American South it would not have been unusual to see a column of slaves, known as a coffle, being walked through the countryside. J. K. Spaulding, Secretary of the Navy under U.S. president Martin van Buren, wrote this eyewitness account:

The sun was shining out very hot, and in turning an angle of the road we encountered the following group: First, a little cart drawn by one horse, in which five or six half-naked black children were tumbled like pigs together. The cart had no covering, and they seemed to have been broiled to sleep. Behind the cart marched three black women, with head, neck and breasts uncovered, and without shoes or stockings; next came three men, bareheaded, half naked and chained together with an ox-chain. Last of all came a white man . . . on horseback, carrying pistols in his belt.[49]

Slavery had a major impact on the Americas as well as Africa. As can be imagined, losing a family member to the slave trade tore families apart and deeply affected social relations. It impacted the economy, as the trade in human beings became a profitable export, and it caused the population of West Africa to decline during the height of the slave trade. Millions of young Africans of reproductive age were captured and sent away from their homes, where they otherwise would have raised families and contributed to society. More men were transported to the Americas than women, causing an imbalance that resulted in increased polygamy in Africa and difficulty finding mates for male slaves in the Americas. The rate of economic development in Africa was, in the long run, profoundly affected by centuries of forced migration.[50] In contrast to about 10 percent of Europeans who returned to Europe, and with the exception of the founding of Liberia by freed slaves in 1821, there was rarely any remigration to Africa.

Besides profit, what else motivated those involved in the slave trade to be so cruel as to steal millions of black Africans from their homes and transport them across an ocean? At least part of the answer is found in the biblical story of the so-called Curse of Ham, which whites interpreted in such a way as to justify slavery. Briefly paraphrased, the Book of Genesis (9:18–25) tells how Noah tilled the soil, planted a vineyard, got drunk on wine, and lay uncovered in his tent. Ham, Noah's son and the father of Canaan, saw his naked father and alerted his two brothers, Shem and Japheth, who then respectfully turned their heads away while covering their father. The verse concludes with a wrathful, eternal, Old Testament curse: "When Noah awoke from his wine, and knew what his youngest son had done to him, he said, 'cursed be Canaan; a slave of slaves shall he be to his brothers.'"[51] Since Ham was thought to have dark skin, some whites misinterpreted the passage to mean that dark-skinned people—that is, Africans—were also cursed and destined to be slaves.

It is, of course, a peculiar interpretation, for it remains unclear why Ham's supposed mistake was so sinful. There is also no mention of skin color in the Curse. Nonetheless, Ham and his son Canaan became associated with Black Africa and the passage was commonly cited in Europe and America as a biblical apology for the slave trade. Today we know differences in appearance and skin color between Africans and Europeans are due to geography and human evolution. Africans have dark features because intense sun produces more protective melanin in the skin. In contrast, Europeans have lighter features because there is less sunlight the farther north one goes. Hundreds of years ago, however, people had little understanding of biology or anthropology and relied for information on the sources they knew best, such as the Old and New Testaments of the Bible.

THE SCRAMBLE FOR AFRICA

As the trans-Atlantic slave trade ended and the practice of slavery itself was prohibited in Europe and the Americas in the course of the nineteenth century, colonialism flourished. In this curious paradox of waning slavery and waxing imperialism, European powers partitioned the whole of the African continent with the goals of solidifying their spheres of influence, exporting raw materials back to Europe, and expanding the global economic market. In the straightforward words of British colonial administer F. D. Lugar (1858–1945), "the partition of Africa was, as we all recognize, due primarily to the economic necessity of increasing the supplies of raw materials and food to meet the needs of the industrialized nations of Europe."[52] The Scramble for Africa, as it came to be known, stands out as one of the most audacious and arrogant plans in European history.[53]

European powers met in Berlin, Germany, from November 1884 until February 1885 in order to establish general principles regarding the colonization of Africa. Fifteen states participated in the Conference: The United States, Germany, Austria, Belgium, Denmark, Spain, France, the United Kingdom, Italy, the Netherlands, Portugal, Russia, Sweden, Norway, and the Ottoman Empire. No African countries were present. Although most diplomats participating in the conference had little knowledge of or firsthand experience in Africa, they proceeded with great pomp and circumstance to partition what they referred to as the

"Dark Continent."[54] Without consulting any Africans, they produced "The General Act of the Conference of Berlin Concerning the Congo," a remarkably brazen document outlining European imperial ambitions. Reminiscent of the false piety of the Spanish *Requerimiento*, it begins with the words "*In the name of Almighty God*" and proceeds to spell out the chief aims of developing "liberty of commerce" and creating a free-trade zone in the Congo basin.[55] The Europeans further claimed their intention was to "watch over" the indigenous populations, suppress slavery, respect freedom of religion, and help Africans "understand and appreciate the advantages of civilization"—all of which turned out to be an outrageous lie.[56] The real aim of the 1885 Berlin Conference was, as the official documents acknowledge, to facilitate the "effective occupation" of the African continent.[57]

Behind the scenes, European powers were warily eyeing each other and aggressively jostling for their share of the colonial spoils. Given the enormity of the plan and the hubris of the diplomats, it is not surprising they failed to achieve the declared goals stated in the General Act, for it never created the envisioned free-trade zone or ensured liberty of commerce. It neither mitigated conflict nor led to respect for the human rights and dignity of the indigenous peoples. Quite the opposite, it hastened the scramble for Africa and led to massive bloodshed. As demonstrated in table 2.2, the French took the lion's share of the continent with more than four million square miles of colonial territory. The British claimed an area stretching from Cairo to the Cape at a time when the sun never set on their empire, while the remaining land (excepting only Liberia and Ethiopia) was divided among Germany, Belgium, Portugal, Italy, and Spain.

Few among the Europeans were as greedy or ruthless as King Leopold II of Belgium. He was king of a small northern European country whose parliament had little interest in colonies, but that did not stop him from claiming control over what he called the Congo Free State. As sovereign ruler and one-man owner of the gigantic colony in the heart of the continent, Leopold used forced African labor to extract ivory, rubber, and other natural resources from his crown colony. Rubber, which was collected from vines in the jungle and used for bicycle and vehicle tires at the turn of the twentieth century, became one of the most profitable raw materials in the world and made Leopold unimaginably rich. Were he alive today he would be a multibillionaire. Yet the

Table 2.2. Political Division of Africa in 1914

	Square Miles
French (Tunisia, Algeria, Morocco, French West Africa, French Congo, French Congo, French Somaliland, Madagascar)	4,086,950
British (Union of South Africa, Basutoland, Bechuanaland, Nyasaland, Rhodesia, British East Africa, Uganda, Zanzibar, Somaliland, Nigeria, Gold Coast, Sierra Leone, Gambia, Egypt, Anglo-Egyptian Sudan)	3,701,411
German (East Africa, South-West Africa, Cameroon, Togoland)	910,150
Belgian (Belgian Congo)	900,000
Portuguese (Guinea, West Africa, East Africa)	787,500
Italian (Eritrea, Italian Somaliland, Libya)	600,000
Spanish (Rio de Oro, Muni River Settlements)	79,800
Independent States (Liberia, Ethiopia)	393,000
Total	11,458,811

Source: Stavrianos, *The World Since 1500* (1971), 380.

process of harvesting and exporting the valuable rubber was so insanely brutal and totally exploitive it caused rebellions among the Congolese and protests among European missionaries. Natives who did not collect enough rubber for King Leopold II were shot to death, whipped or— the preferred punishment—had their right hand chopped off.

Adam Hochschild recounts many of these atrocities in *King Leopold's Ghost: A Story of Greed, Terror, and Heroism in Colonial Africa*. "When a village or district failed to supply its quota of rubber or fought back against the regime," he writes, "Force Publique soldiers or rubber company 'sentries' often killed everyone they could find. Those times when an eyewitness happened upon a pile of skeletons or severed hands, and a report survives, represent, of course, only a small proportion of the massacres carried out, only a few sparks from a firestorm."[58] A small but representative sample of the written accounts of the murder, rape, and pillage that occurred in the Congo include the following: An 1896 newspaper report stated that 1,308 severed African hands were delivered to a colonial District Commissioner named Léon Fiévez in a single day. A Swedish missionary named E. V. Sjöblom came across a lake full of dead bodies with their right hands missing and explained: "when I crossed the stream I saw some dead bodies hanging down from the branches in the water. As I turned away my face at the horrible sight one of the native corporals who was following us down said 'Oh, that is nothing, a few days ago I returned from a fight, and I brought the white man 160 hands and they were thrown into the river.'"[59] An English explorer named Ewart S. Grogan reported while walking through the northeastern Congo that "every village has been burnt to the ground, and as I fled from the country I saw skeletons, skeletons everywhere; and such postures—what tales of horror they told!"[60] As a result of all this savagery, the population of the Congo dropped by approximately 50 percent and an estimated 10 million Congolese died during King Leopold's nearly three-decade reign. In an attempt to destroy the evidence of his deeds, he had the Congo Free State archives destroyed before turning the territory over to the Belgian state in 1908.

Joseph Conrad captured the essence of these crimes in his classic novella *Heart of Darkness* (1899).[61] Conrad himself had gone to Africa in 1890 planning to pilot a steamboat up the Congo River, but the plan fell through upon his arrival and he was forced to return in ill health to England. The experience affected him deeply, though, and led to what became a popular and widely read book on the effects of European colonialism. *Heart of Darkness* depicts a man named Charles Marlow, who while sitting Buddha-style in a boat on the Thames in London, recounts to his friends a trip up the Congo he once made in search of a Belgian ivory trader named Mr. Kurtz. Marlow's description of Africa is dark, beautiful, and mysterious, and his portrayal of European colonialism is harsh and damning. "The conquest of the earth," he says, involves robbery, violence, and murder and "mostly means the taking it away from those who have a different complexion or slightly flatter noses than ourselves."[62] When Marlow finds Kurtz living in the jungle at the end of the river, he is left with the madman's delirious, haunting last words, "The horror! The horror!"[63] The novella ends back in London with the Thames, the great conduit of globalization, described as "the tranquil waterway leading to the uttermost ends of the earth," flowing somberly "into the heart of an immense darkness."[64] Conrad's stirring novella is now interpreted as a powerful literary critique of the worst excesses of imperialism at its nineteenth-century zenith.

By the start of the twentieth century European traders, explorers, missionaries, kings, and colonialists had penetrated Africa and integrated the continent into the global economic market. Natural resources such as ivory, rubber, gold, wood, palm oil, and cotton were extracted as efficiently as possible and exported to Europe and the rest of the world. This entailed establishing trading posts, protecting colonial markets from other European competitors, building railroads, and navigating steamships up rivers and across oceans. As Europe headed into the abyss of World War I, nearly all of Africa had been colonized.

FROM COLONIALISM TO NEOCOLONIALISM

A basic tenet of the relationship between wealthy core states and impoverished peripheral states is that "the strength of the state-machinery in core states is a function of the weakness of other state machineries. Hence intervention of outsiders via war, subversion, and diplomacy is the lot of peripheral states."[65] Even a cursory look back through the last few centuries reveals a virtually interminable list of core state interventions in the affairs of weak peripheral states, of the strong preying on the weak. As we have seen in Africa, the immediate, short-term consequences of outside economic and military intervention were, in most cases, devastating for the native inhabitants. The long-term consequences were no different. In the Congo, the specter of King Leopold haunted the country decades after his death, literally, as the belief spread that he had been reincarnated in the form of a powerful Catholic Bishop named Jean-Félix de Hemptinne and was responsible for a wide range of injustices and calamities. As Hochschild concludes, the historical legacy of slavery and colonialism has been "authoritarian rule and plunder. On the whole continent, perhaps no nation has had a harder time than the Congo in emerging from the shadow of its past. When independence finally came to the Congo, the country fared badly."[66] Today's Democratic Republic of the Congo is racked by ethnic conflict that rages on year after year. More than five million people died in a civil war there from 1998 to 2007, and amputating limbs is still a form of punishment.[67]

The pattern of colonial rule ending badly repeats itself, again and again, around the world. In Vietnam, Laos, and Cambodia, French colonialists tried to carry out what they called a "civilizing mission," which was merely another form of expanding the market for their goods, reinforcing cultural dominance, and exploiting the region. Heavy-handed French overlords established massive rice and rubber plantations, used the locals for cheap labor, and exported the raw materials. When nationalist resistance grew after World War II, the French lost 90,000 men trying in vain to hold on to Indochina. When the French let go, the United States took up the imperialist mantle in

Vietnam and began a decade-long war that ultimately killed more than a million people. Among the many negative consequences of the war was an exodus of hundreds of thousands of so-called Vietnamese Boat People, refugees who fled in desperation on rickety, overcrowded boats into the South China Sea.

Turning from Africa and Asia to Central America reveals a familiar story in a different setting. In Nicaragua, for instance, the terrible legend of a man named William Walker still haunts the country and the wider region. In the mid-nineteenth century, men such as Walker—and there were many of them—were called filibusters, a term used to describe mercenaries who made war and wreaked havoc in Central America with the goal of establishing new colonies, exploiting the local inhabitants, and getting rich. Walker was born in Tennessee and had studied medicine in both the United States and Europe, but he yearned for adventure and so organized a series of expeditions into Central America that made him the "most notorious filibuster of the nineteenth century."[68] He attempted first to colonize the Baja California Peninsula in 1853, but failed. In 1855 he and a group of mercenary soldiers, mostly veterans from the 1846–1848 Mexican-American War, were invited to Nicaragua to fight on behalf of the Liberals who were trying to oust the ruling Conservatives. He and fifty-seven men, calling themselves "The Immortals," proceeded to capture what was then the capital city of Granada. He soon took command of the army, appointed himself president, legalized slavery, and declared English the official language. He had visions of conquering all of Central America, but was overthrown in 1857 and forced to return to the United States. Walker's final filibuster ended in Honduras in September 1860 when he was captured by British and Honduran authorities and put to death in front of a firing squad.[69]

This tale of invasion and violence, war and chaos, aggression and imperialism foreshadowed much of what was to come and set the stage for a series of U.S. interventions in Nicaragua and elsewhere in Central America. In 1912, for instance, U.S. Marines landed in Nicaragua to protect the interests of U.S. companies there and help the conservative regime of Adolfo Díaz. The presence of foreign troops created resistance among the people, including a man named Augusto César Sandino. When U.S. Marines returned to Nicaragua again in 1927, Sandino and his followers—known as Sandinistas—established a guerilla army in the mountainous northern part of the country and waged war against both the U.S. Marines and the conservative government it was propping up. Sandino's attitude was defiant: "Now I want you to come and disarm me. . . . you will not make me cede by any other means. I am not for sale. I do not give up."[70] By the time Anastasio Somoza's National Guard murdered Sandino in 1934 he had won the support of the poor, peasants, workers, and indigenous people and achieved cult status in Central America.

Somoza took control of Nicaragua in 1936 and ruled the country as a military dictator for twenty years until he was assassinated. He was the son of a coffee plantation owner and had gone to school as a boy in Philadelphia, Pennsylvania, spoke perfect English, and was generally pro-American, all of which helped him win the steady backing of the United States. He was greedy, corrupt, and ruthless—but he was not a communist, and that is what mattered most to the United States. Dubbed "el yanqui" by the Americans, he allowed U.S.-based corporations to extract the country's natural resources, exploit the workers, and make off with the profits. President Roosevelt famously summed up the relationship with Somoza by saying he was "a son of a bitch, but our son of a bitch."[71] Somoza himself later acknowledged that "over a period of years, we sent over fourteen thousand men through various military training programs in the United States . . . Due to our close association with the U.S., Nicaragua was often referred to as 'the little U.S.A.' of Central America."[72] Somoza was assassinated by the poet Rigoberto Lopez Pérez in 1956, but his sons Luis and Anastasio Jr. (a graduate of the U.S. Military Academy West Point) continued the family dynasty's rule and remained subservient to the United States until the Sandinista National Liberation Front finally ousted the Somozas in 1979.

The Sandinistas took a stance that defied U.S. hegemony and immediately began a series of reforms aimed at helping the poor and minimizing inequality. They took land from the Somoza family, who had previously been the largest private landowners in the country, and redistributed it to the peasants. They raised the minimum wage and recognized workers' unions, collective bargaining, and the right to strike—rights that workers in the United States and Europe had also fought long and hard for. They built schools and expanded educational programs, health care, and women's rights. Normally these are seen as positive developments, but U.S. president Ronald Reagan considered the Sandinistas to be communists and therefore supported the *contras*, a rebel group fighting the Sandinistas. In a particularly deadly scheme, the United States illegally sold weapons to Iran and funneled money made from the deal to the *contra* rebels in Nicaragua. Infamous U.S. colonel Oliver North took the fall for the Reagan administration's criminal financing of the *contras*, which became known as the Iran-Contra Scandal, but was let off the hook with a slap on the wrist. (Today Mr. North is regarded by the right wing in the United States as a type of hero-patriot. He can be found glorifying militarism in his weekly show "War Stories" on the *Fox News* television channel.[73]) In the end, an estimated 30,000 Nicaraguans died in the Contra War. In 1990, a new conservative government came to power under Violeta Chamorro that was much more sympathetic to the United States and its neoliberal economic policies.

Philip Agee, a former CIA agent who witnessed and participated in much of the United States meddling in Central America, said the 1970s was a time "when the worst imaginable horrors were going on in Latin America. Argentina, Brazil, Chile, Uruguay, Paraguay, Guatemala, El Salvador—they were military dictatorships with death squads, all with the backing of the CIA and the US government."[74] But why? Why would the United States support oppressive regimes, take the side of military dictators, and interfere in the affairs of so many countries? Agee adroitly concluded in a tell-all book entitled *Inside the Company: CIA Diary* that the United States did it in order to preserve "property relations and other institutions on which rest the interests of our own wealthy and privileged minority."[75] That is to say, it was done to uphold the world-economy and the dominance of the United States.

It is important to understand that war is the most terrible form of outside intervention. War is the most insidious aspect of globalization, worse even than economic inequality and ecological destruction (all of which are interconnected). It is the great enemy of our collective well-being, for not only does it poison the minds of the soldiers who are sent off to kill and be killed, it drives people from their homes. As we have seen in places like Vietnam and Iraq, war produces refugees, asylum seekers, and stateless persons. The result of military invasions, regardless of where they happen, is usually increased poverty, internal strife, and emigration. One can only imagine what would happen if the tables were turned and a powerful foreign country meddled in American, French, or Belgian politics, plundered national resources, cut off people's hands, overthrew democratically elected leaders, and killed masses of people. If 30,000 Americans or millions of Europeans died in a war financed by outsiders, there would be public outrage and disgust at the injustice of it. There would be cries for the perpetrators to be brought to justice and no end to the retribution and restitution demanded by the victims' families.

CONCLUSION

Migration has occurred since the beginning of our origins in Africa millions of years ago. It is as old as humanity itself and played an integral role in the spread of culture and civilization. While tracing migration back in time can seem like an infinite regress, the era of European exploration marks an important point in history when globalization and migration converged in a significant way. Historically, exploration has been a precursor to conquest. The Vikings reached North America and left oral records of their travels that were later written down, but they were ahead of their time. The Spaniards, by contrast, had the technology and know-how to navigate the globe. They also knew what they wanted and few articulated it more clearly than Christopher Columbus himself. "Gold is most excellent; gold constitutes treasure," he wrote in a July 1503 letter to the King and Queen of Spain, "and he who has it does all he wants in the world, and can even lift souls up to Paradise."[76] Expressed in a thousand different ways since, this sentiment captured the essential motivation of the conquistadors, colonialists, and neo-imperialists who followed.

Capitalism expanded from the sixteenth century onward from its core in Western Europe to peripheral regions in the Americas, Africa, and Asia. Within the context of expanding economic markets, the largest transoceanic migration in human history occurred when Europeans left their overcrowded, impoverished circumstances and settled the New World. It was an enormous migration that marked a transcontinental shift in labor and was critical to making the United States part of the hegemonic core of the capitalist world-economy. Easily the cruelest and most unjust form of migration during this expansionary period was the transportation of slaves from Africa to the Americas. Forced labor was an integral part of the Industrial Revolution in the eighteenth and nineteenth centuries, as slaves were exploited in order to keep the supply of raw materials flowing from the Americas to Europe. Cotton picked by slaves on plantations in the American South, for example, was sent to be processed in textile factories where poor Britons worked in hellish conditions. Cloth and other finished products were then sold to a growing number of consumers in an ever-expanding market.

Colonialism ended in the twentieth century, but neocolonialism remained. In a noteworthy twist of modern history, most colonized countries rejected colonialism but remained within the capitalist world-economy. Core countries maintained their political, economic, and sociocultural hegemony, as compliant governments and corrupt elites in peripheral countries allowed multinational corporations to continue extracting natural resources. The capitalist world-system, characterized by an international division of labor and an unequal exchange of goods that reinforced the economic development of core countries and underdevelopment of peripheral countries, stayed firmly in place. Not surprisingly, people dislocated by exploitation and war associated with the penetration of the global economic market into peripheral areas of the Global South were compelled to migrate both internally and internationally. In other words, the empire came home.

CHAPTER 3

THE GLOBAL SOUTH

Photographer Don Bartletti and journalist Sonia Nazario went to Mexico in the summer of 2000 to chronicle the lives of children riding atop the Beast, the foreboding name given to crime-ridden freight trains heading toward the United States. Bartletti and Nazario both won Pulitzer Prizes for their six-part series in the *Los Angeles Times* entitled "Enrique's Journey—The Boy Left Behind."[1] The articles and subsequent best-selling book by Nazario tell the true story of Enrique, a five-year-old who is left behind in Honduras and at sixteen sets out to find his mother in the United States. On his eighth attempt he manages to cross the Rio Grande River on an inner tube and is finally reunited, although the untreated psychological trauma of his childhood leaves him struggling to cope with life in America. In a larger sense, the story is about all the girls and boys looking for missing parents who have gone north.

In the small Mexican town of Tapachula near the Guatemalan border Don Bartletti met Denis Contreras, a twelve-year-old Honduran boy traveling toward the United States, alone, in search of his mother. "I want to see my mother because I don't know her. I want to see her face. She lives in the state of Los Angeles," said little Denis, holding out a scrap of paper with her phone number on it.[2] Denis was one of thousands of Central American children looking for parents, mothers in particular, who had made the heart-wrenching decision to leave their children behind. He was among the many who wanted to ask simple questions, like "Why did you leave?" and "Do you love me?"

In the years since Enrique and Denis rode the Beast through Mexico, the number of kids under the age of eighteen making the same dangerous trip has grown dramatically—into the tens of thousands every year. In 2011, U.S. authorities apprehended 15,949 unaccompanied children at the Mexico-U.S. border, and in 2014 that number had ballooned to 68,551.[3] Nearly all come from El Salvador, Guatemala, Honduras—known as the Northern Triangle—and Mexico, and are fleeing various forms of poverty, mistreatment, and gang violence. They are leaving dangerous situations they can no longer tolerate.

Yet the long thousand-mile journey through Mexico to the United States is extremely dangerous, particularly for an unaccompanied child. Running alongside and jumping onto a moving cargo train is hard to do, and if you slip and fall you could get a leg crushed ferociously under the screeching wheels of the train, or you could die. Once you are on the roof of the Beast, which is also referred to as the "Death Train," there is no rail to hold on to. If a tunnel appears, you must lay down flat and try not to get hit. If the train suddenly changes speed or jerks to one side, you have to keep yourself from getting hurled off. Then there are corrupt police, gangs, and the mafia who brutalize migrants in general, but prey in particular on children and commit all manner of unspeakable crimes against them. They are cheated, robbed, beaten, kidnapped, extorted, held for ransom, recruited into gangs, raped, forced into prostitution, and killed. Sergio Mercado, a seventeen-year-old Honduran, said of his experience riding the Beast: "I encountered gang members armed with guns and machetes. I saw the gangs kill three people, shooting them or shoving them off the train . . . the gangs communicate by cell phone, and know which ones paid and which ones still owe them."[4] Kids who survive the journey physically are often psychologically traumatized for life, and finding a parent who abandoned them offers as much potential heartbreak as joy.

When Denis Contreras found his mother in San Diego, California, it was not an easy transition. He did go to school, but also got in trouble with the law, and his mother sent him back to Honduras. He returned again to the United States, but was eventually deported. In 2014 Don Bartletti traveled to Honduras—a country with one of the highest murder rates in the world—and interviewed twenty-six-year-old Denis, now a husband and father, in his home city of San Pedro Sula:

> Do you wish you'd never gone?—Yes.
> But you found your real mom, learned English, and got a job. That was your dream on the train. Wasn't that good enough?—No.
> What would you say to those thousands of kids who want to ride the trains to the North now?—I would tell them to stay. They might get a better life, but if God wanted them to be born in the United States, he would have done that. He decided for us to live right here.[5]

Millions of migrant children such as Enrique, Denis, and Sergio come not only from Central America, but also South America, Africa, Asia, the Middle East, and everywhere there are large numbers of people on the move. They are innocent victims of an economic and political system that has produced grinding poverty, failed states, and war. In short, they are casualties of the downside of globalization.

As illustrated in the preceding chapter, the expansion of the capitalist market into peripheral regions initiates and perpetuates international migration. The mechanisms that initiate the dislocation of people include appropriating land, extracting natural resources, and disrupting traditional ways of life. When colonialism ended in the second half of the twentieth century, the dislocation continued under neocolonialism and corporate capitalism. With this conceptual framework in mind, let us turn to the Global South, which includes most of Asia, Africa, and Latin America.

MEXICO AND NAFTA

Mexico provides a rich case study of the nexus between globalization and migration. The country can be used to demonstrate neoclassical economic theories that suggest wage differentials are a leading cause of international migration. That is, people in countries where there is a surplus of labor and low wages, such as Mexico, migrate to countries that need workers and offer more money, such as the United States and Canada. Alternatively, the Mexican case provides evidence to support the family (or household) theory of migration, which asserts that the decision to move abroad is due to more than just wage differentials. It involves a series of complex cost-benefit calculations made by the family unit in order to survive economically in an interconnected, interdependent world. Mexican migration to the United States also illustrates network theory, which proposes that migrants form social, economic, and cultural networks that strengthen ties between the country of origin and country of destination, which results in yet more migration. The same is true for segmented labor theory, whereby international migration is viewed as the result of government policies designed to actively recruit and attract guest workers, such as the Bracero Program that brought hundreds of thousands of Mexicans to the United States.[6]

Considered a semi-peripheral country, Mexico lies on the great fault line between the Global North and South. With a population of 125 million it is the second largest country in Latin America, after Brazil. It has a relatively high birthrate of 2.27 births per woman and a population projected to reach 140 million by mid-century.[7] In 2015, Mexicans made up the largest single group of immigrants in the United States, with nearly twelve million residing there legally and another six million illegally.[8] The question is, why did they leave their homes and start anew in the North? The answer involves a combination of socioeconomic, political, and historical factors.

European intervention in Mexico dates back to the arrival of the Spanish conquistadors in the sixteenth century. From the beginning, the invasion was spectacularly audacious, ruthless, and exploitive. When Hernán Cortés—described by Eduardo Galeano as one of many Renaissance Europeans who "ventured across the ocean and buried their teeth in the throats of the Indian civilizations"—arrived in 1519 in what is now the Mexican state of Veracruz, he deliberately sank his ships so the expedition could not turn back.[9] Thereafter, his six hundred men stopped talking mutiny and started working together to conquer the Aztec Empire of Montezuma II. This set the stage for several hundred years of Spanish colonialism, followed by American intervention from

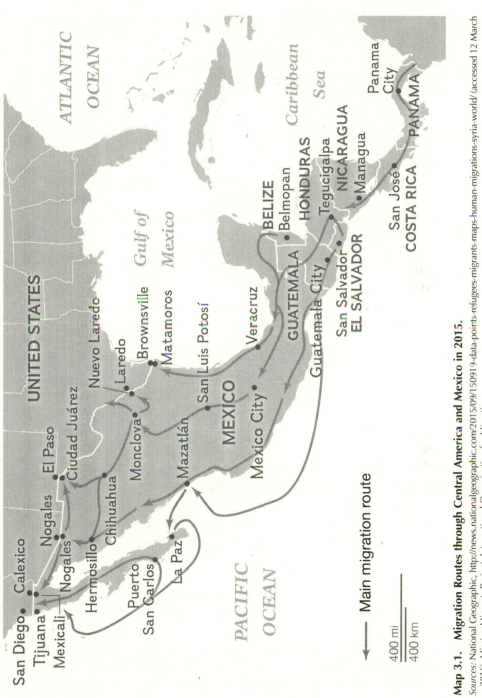

Map 3.1. Migration Routes through Central America and Mexico in 2015.

Sources: National Geographic, http://news.nationalgeographic.com/2015/09/150919-data-points-refugees-migrants-maps-human-migrations-syria-world/ (accessed 12 March 2016); Missing Migrants Project, International Organization for Migration.

the mid-nineteenth century onward. Hence, the political economy of Mexico has long been inextricably intertwined with that of Spain and Europe, the United States and North America.

The southwestern United States was part of the Spanish colony of New Spain and then, after Mexican independence in 1821, part of Mexico. The United States annexed Texas in 1845 and went to war with Mexico from 1846 to 1848 to gain what are now the states of Arizona, California, Colorado, Nevada, New Mexico, Utah, and Wyoming. Vehement protests from the likes of Henry David Thoreau and Abraham Lincoln, who argued that the Mexican-American War was an unjust act of aggression, did not stop the United States from taking nearly half of Mexico's territory. Approximately 100,000 Spanish speakers who lived in this massive area in 1848 were given the choice to relocate to Mexico or become Americans, and about 90 percent chose the latter. This is why the idea persists among Spanish speakers in places like the U.S. state of New Mexico—where nearly half the population is Hispanic—that they did not cross the border, rather it crossed them. As the United States expanded militarily across the continent, the U.S. economy expanded into Mexico as well.

Mexicans had been recruited to work in the United States in the nineteenth and early twentieth centuries, but the Mexican-U.S. Program of the Loan of Laborers, commonly called the Bracero Program, ushered in a new era of labor migration between the countries.[10] In order to fill a labor shortage in the United States during World War II, Mexican guest workers called "braceros" (a Spanish term for manual labor, or literally "someone who works with his arms") came to the United States to do mostly unskilled work in the agricultural sector. The first agreement was signed between the U.S. and Mexican governments in 1942 at a time when the United States had conscripted much of its young male population and put people to work in weapons factories. The original plan called for Mexican men—women were not allowed to participate in the program—to work in the United States and return to Mexico when their contracts expired. In 1944, some 62,000 Mexicans came to the United States and between 1942 and 1947 a total of 219,000 worked in twenty-four American states.[11] When the United States wanted to renew the Bracero Program in 1948, Mexico was initially reluctant to lose so many of its workers and refused to continue the program. In response, the United States simply opened its southern border and allowed thousands of braceros to enter.

The Korean War caused another labor shortage in the United States, which led to the Bracero Program's renewal in 1951. The subsequent large-scale migration of Mexican guest workers was at times contentious. In February 1954 the Mexican government of Adolfo Ruiz Cortines sent troops to the border in order to prevent the exodus of unauthorized emigrants. When economic recession struck that same year the Eisenhower administration implemented "Operation Wetback," a paramilitary program aimed at stopping illegal immigration and deporting undocumented Mexicans. ("Wetback" refers to the wet backs of undocumented migrants wading and swimming across the Rio Grande River and is now, depending on the user and context, considered either a derogatory term or positive identifier.) Thus, policies on both sides of the border were at times chaotic and contradictory—much like the larger process of globalization—with the Mexican government sending and then trying to stop labor migrants, and the U.S. government variously recruiting Mexicans and deporting them. In hindsight, it is clear that American farmers benefited immensely from the large reserve of cheap labor that could be called up at any time. Mexicans were promised the prevailing wage for their work, but that was always low, which in turn depressed the pay of manual laborers and poor people and undercut organized labor unions in the United States.

After the Bracero Program ended in 1964, the pattern of migration nevertheless continued as Mexicans entered the United States with or without the proper documents. Going north to work in the United States became customary, expected, and even part of the culture. The pattern of migration and settlement had been initiated, and social networks on both sides of the border perpetuated the process. Many Mexicans who came to the United States under the Bracero Program preferred to stay and have their families join them rather than return home. This emigration deeply affected rural Mexico in a multitude of economic and social ways. So many men went north that some rural villages were comprised primarily of women, children, and the elderly. As the years and decades passed, the extent of border security along the 1,954-mile U.S.-Mexican border increased, so that what once was a circular pattern of seasonal migration became harder due to increased border control and law enforcement. Crossing back and forth grew increasingly difficult, dangerous, and expensive, which led to migrants staying in the United States rather than returning to Mexico and risking the dangerous journey again.

Migration songs called *migra corridos* were (and continue to be) sung about leaving home, crossing the border, working abroad, racism, leaving loved ones behind, and many other topics. "Beautiful Borders," "The Dishwasher" and "This Wetback is Dry" offer an illustrative sampling of some of the migrant ballad titles and their themes. The 1981 satirical *corrido* "Superman is Illegal" goes like this: "It's a bird; it's a plane; no, it's a wetback" and depicts Superman as an undocumented worker in the United States. The singer-narrator tells the Border Patrol that even though Superman is blond and blue-eyed, he is still an illegal alien from the planet Krypton and should not be working. Besides, he is not into serving in the U.S. military, has not paid taxes, and does not have a green card or a license to fly.[12] Another *corrido* includes a salty cross-border dialogue between an American chorus that sings "Don't call me gringo, you fuckin' beaner; stay on your side of that goddamn river" and a Mexican one that counters "Don't call me beaner, Mr. Asshole; I'll scare you for being a racist and an asshole."[13] The songs articulate a wide variety of psychosocial aspects of international migration, which are often difficult to separate from the political and economic.

To reiterate, globalization is a set of processes that "stretches social, political, and economic activities across political frontiers, regions, and continents. It intensifies our dependence on each other, as flows of trade, investment, finance, migration, and culture increase."[14] Few things exemplify this description of globalization as well as the North American Free Trade Agreement (NAFTA) between Canada, the United States, and Mexico. Along with the World Bank, World Trade Organization (WTO), and International Monetary Fund (IMF), NAFTA has played a key role in the expansion of neoliberal economic policies pushed by the United States. As Leo Panitch and Sam Gindin note in *The Making of Global Capitalism: The Political Economy of American Empire*, NAFTA was a mechanism used to extend "capitalism as a global project" and to "reinforce the material and ideological conditions for international legal rules guaranteeing free trade."[15]

In effect since January 1994, NAFTA allows for the free movement of goods and capital among the three countries. Yet, unlike the European Union and its Schengen Area—another quintessential illustration of globalization—it does not allow for the free movement of people. Ironically, its original purpose was to mitigate poverty, increase foreign direct investment, and promote fair competition. The preamble to the agreement claims its goals are to "improve working conditions and living standards," undertake "environmental protection and conservation," "promote sustainable development," and "protect, enhance and enforce basic workers' rights."[16] In the decades since it was implemented, however, its main effect on Mexico has instead been economic crisis, job loss, poverty, pollution, and emigration. How did this happen, especially when the stated intent of NAFTA was to economically develop rather than underdevelop Mexico?

Much of the answer has to do with the inherently unequal core-periphery relationship between the United States and Canada on one side, and Mexico on the other. Under NAFTA, the number of mostly U.S. and Canadian companies that set up factories just over the border in Mexico increased dramatically. Assembly plants known as maquiladoras (*maquilar* means "to assemble" in Spanish) had existed since 1965 when the Mexican government tried to increase industrialization along its northern border, but their numbers grew dramatically in the mid-1990s. By 1999, roughly 4,000 maquiladoras employed more than one million Mexicans, most of whom earned between $3.50 and $5.00 per day.[17] In essence, the system allows foreign-owned and operated companies to register in Mexico in order to take advantage of the cheap, abundant labor. They import raw materials that are assembled in Mexico and export the finished products back to places like the United States and Canada. It is a classic example of what economists call the "externalization of costs," whereby Mexico pays the real human and ecological costs of production while the profits are sent abroad. Because social conditions surrounding the maquiladoras are so wretched, and the polluted environment around them is hazardous to people's health, they ultimately do more harm than good.

Part of the problem is that maquiladoras compete with sweatshop factories in Asia. In order to compete in this international race to the bottom, costs are kept low, lax environmental laws are flouted, and safety regulations are held to a minimum. Even when Mexican laws stipulate workers should get such things as vacation time, maternity leave, and severance pay, unscrupulous factory managers ignore them with impunity. Martha Ojeda, a Mexican woman who worked for twenty years in a maquiladora, said that "workers labor from sunrise to sunset. They never see day light. They are sometimes exposed to toxic chemicals, and in one case workers were given 'vitamins' which turned out to be amphetamines. They rarely see their families; often wives will work for one shift, then switch with their husbands who take the next shift."[18] The end effect on Mexican society is poverty and inequality.

As Timothy Wise, Hilda Salazar, and Laura Carlsen have demonstrated in *Confronting Globalization: Economic Integration and Popular Resistance in Mexico*, the social and environmental costs of NAFTA have been high and the economic benefits low. The consequences for Mexico have been almost entirely negative, including the following: (1) While job growth has occurred, it has not been accompanied by higher standards of living or better working or environmental conditions—quite the opposite. The number of jobs produced appears large, but falls far short of the number actually needed for the whole country. (2) The maquiladora model is overly dependent on the cycles of the U.S. economy and thus vulnerable to crash based on the whims of outside investors. (3) Since most materials are imported from abroad and the finished products and profits exported, few of the industries are sustainable in the long run. The result is economic instability. (4) The prevalence of female workers in the plants has compounded the exploitation, in part because of discrimination and the status of women in a patriarchal Mexican society. (5) Lastly, there is the significant cost of "the expulsion of large numbers of people from their communities and, in the absence of viable employment in other sectors of the economy, their country. The current model for liberalization is particularly cruel for these workers. While goods and capital travel ever more freely across borders, restrictions on Mexican migration to the Unites States become more severe."[19] To sum it up, economic globalization has been harmful to Mexico and its people.

In the words of local community organizer Ignacio del Valle, "the concept of globalization has hit hard. Right in the face. The system no longer hides what's behind it. It openly says 'I'll take your land and exploit you.'"[20] In large measure, this visceral, bare-knuckles description of what NAFTA has done to Mexico is the result of what economist Arghiri Emmanuel identified in the 1950s as "unequal exchange." When wealthy countries such as Canada and the United States exchange products that have high labor costs—like a bulldozer—for products made in Mexico that have low labor costs—say, a large shipment of denim blue jeans—there is a transfer of profit, or surplus value, from the periphery to the core. It is also the result of unequal terms of trade tucked away in the fine print of the agreement. For instance, American farmers continued to get government subsidies under NAFTA, while tariffs that had once protected Mexican agriculture were cut. As a result, the Mexicans could no longer sell their corn as cheaply as big American agribusiness, which flooded the Mexican market with foreign corn and put small farmers out of business.

Why, then, did the Mexican government enter into NAFTA if the consequences have been overwhelmingly adverse? Many of Mexico's business and political leaders were educated at elite universities in the United States, where they were not only taught the logic of neoliberal economic policy but implemented it with vigor when they returned home and rose to power. Take Miguel de la Madrid Hurtado, who in 1965 earned a masters degree in public administration from Harvard University.[21] As president of Mexico (1982–1988) he left a legacy of privatization and economic austerity measures. His successor, Carlos Salinas de Gortari, earned a PhD in political economy from Harvard University in 1978.[22] President Salinas (1988–1994) cut social programs, denationalized Mexican banks, allowed foreign firms to drill for oil in Mexico, pushed hard for NAFTA, and saw the standard of living decline for the working class. President Ernesto Zedillo (1994–2000) got a PhD in economics from Yale University and—what else?—embraced economic globalization. When Zedillo devalued the Mexican peso against the U.S. dollar in 1994, the currency crashed, inflation rose by 50 percent annually, and up to a million Mexicans lost their jobs.[23] President Vicente Fox (2000–2006) got a graduate degree in management from Harvard before becoming an executive at Coca-Cola, which led critics to say he was trying to run the country like a soft-drink company.[24] The list goes on, but suffice it to say Mexico has had a long succession of Ivy League–educated leaders who compliantly pursued neoliberal economic policies that favor corporations.

The crucial point is that these presidents, their advisors and the esteemed universities that educated them all represent a powerful mechanism—the pervasive "ideological commitment to the system as a whole"—that upholds the capitalist world-economy and enables it to continue.[25] In other words, Mexican elites dedicated themselves to the principles of trade liberalization, free financial flows, deregulation, and privatization. They rose to power and stayed there, by hook or crook, arguing that Mexico was vested in the free market system and that everyone's livelihood depended on its continuation. In the process, they looted the country and defrauded the people on a grand scale. In an orgy of corruption they helped one of their own, billionaire Carlos Slim Helú, emerge as the richest man in the world. Slim amassed a fortune of 59 billion dollars in 2007 and was, for a time, richer than Bill Gates. He usurped his billions when President Salinas sold him the national telephone company, Telmex, and allowed him to monopolize the industry. This fortune came at the expense of the Mexican population as a whole, but especially the poor, women, and children.

Today every second Mexican lives in poverty and every sixth in extreme poverty. One-quarter of the population is underemployed and for those who have work, wages are comparatively low (the minimum wage in 2014 was 60 cents an hour, or about $5 a day).[26] As forty-two-year-old maquiladora worker Marisela Martínez put it, "sometimes I ask myself: Why to work so much for so little? This is a life in darkness. Once, we run out of gas and we had to eat tortillas with salt for three days until we gathered the money."[27] It is no wonder hard-working people like Marisela pick up and head north to the United States, where they can earn ten times more money than in Mexico.

CENTRAL AMERICA AND CAFTA

Guatemala, Honduras, and El Salvador comprise the so-called Northern Triangle of Central America and are noteworthy due to the high number of their citizens who have migrated north. Particularly striking is the number of child migrants fleeing these countries and traveling on freight trains alone through Mexico toward the United States. Of the three, Guatemala stands out as a classic case study of globalization and its many discontents.

Guatemala's population of 15 million is the largest among the Central American countries (Mexico is Latin American but geographically part of North America). It also has the highest fertility rate at 2.9 children per woman, the highest population growth rate at more than 1.8 percent, and the youngest overall population with a median age of 21.[28] The population is approximately 60 percent Indian, making it one of a small number of Latin American countries that is majority indigenous. More than half of all Guatemalans and nearly three-quarters of the indigenous Mayan population live in poverty; women and children are hit particularly hard and suffer from high rates of mortality. According to the United Nations Children's Fund (UNICEF), in 2010 half of all Guatemalan children under five years of age and over 80 percent of indigenous children suffered from chronic malnutrition.[29]

As in all Central American countries, Guatemala's politics have been influenced heavily by its tumultuous colonial history. It was a Spanish colony for almost three hundred years, during which time Europeans took control of the country's resources, established large plantations, and exploited the indigenous peoples. Land previously farmed by Guatemalan peasants was expropriated and consolidated, and a small elite profited from the work of the masses as coffee, bananas, and sugar became the dominant crops and main exports of the country. After Guatemala gained independence from Spain in 1821, the patterns of economic exploitation and political repression continued. Bitter civil wars, assassinations, military dictatorships, and violent struggle between political factions were the norm for much of the nineteenth and twentieth centuries. In such a political climate, indigenous peasants fared poorly against a small governing elite that was sympathetic to foreign companies.

The United Fruit Company, today called Chiquita, was among the first multinational corporations to do business in Guatemala. Founded in 1899 by three Americans—Lorenzo Dow Baker, Andrew Preston, and Minor Keith—United Fruit became an important actor in international trade and commerce. It came to be known throughout Latin America as "The Octopus" because it was such a dominant, imperialist, anti-union economic force and seemingly had its tentacles everywhere. By the early 1900s it owned thousands of acres of land, a fleet of more than a hundred ships, and hundreds of miles of railroad in Central America. But when Guatemalan presidents Juan José Arévelo (1945–1950) and Jacobo Arbenz (1951–1954) implemented genuine reforms—such as ending the forced labor of indigenous Guatemalans, introducing a minimum wage, and redistributing land to the peasants—United Fruit appealed to the U.S. government for help. Being the largest landowner in the country, it feared having land redistributed back to the Guatemalan people. As a result, the U.S. Central Intelligence Agency (CIA) intervened in 1954 and helped overthrow the democratically elected government of Jacobo Arbenz. The CIA handpicked Arbenz's ardently

anticommunist successor, Colonel Carlos Castillo Armas, who immediately undid the earlier reforms and in the process killed and exiled
thousands of his opponents. The killing occurred in a merciless and
brazen manner, as masses of people were shot or simply disappeared
and never seen again. Thereafter, an elite class of military leaders and
wealthy landowners solidified political and economic control of the
country, leaving landless peasants little choice but to work on plantations or move to the city, where they often lived in slums.

Guatemala's military dictatorships—that of notorious war criminal
General Ríos Montt, who was president from 1982–1983, is a good
case in point—needed U.S. backing and support in order to stay in
power. They readily got it from McCarthy- and Vietnam-era militant
enthusiasts in the United States willing to help rightist Guatemalan
governments put down peasant rebellions and quash any public opposition. The United States Department of War (renamed the Department of Defense in 1949) trained Latin American military leaders at the
infamous School of the Americas at Fort Gulick in the Panama Canal
Zone and later at Fort Benning, Georgia, allegedly to fight commu-
nism in Latin America. In a statement typical of early 1960s Cold War
paranoia, President Kennedy said "the most critical spot on the globe
nowadays is Latin America, which seems made-to-order for the Communists.[30] One result of U.S. counterinsurgency efforts, interventions,
and military support for Guatemalan dictators was a prolonged thirty-
six-year civil war lasting from 1960 to 1996 that claimed the lives of
an estimated 200,000 people. This, in brief, is the graphic backstory of
the large-scale international migration of Guatemalans to Mexico, the
United States, and Canada.

An estimated 1.5 million Guatemalans—approximately 10 percent
of the country's total population—live in the United States. They have
emigrated in large part due to the chaos, criminality, and lawlessness that
resulted from the decades-long civil war and ensuing drug war that has
engulfed much of Latin America in recent years. Crime and gang violence
are now so out of hand that hired assassins charge only twenty dollars
per murder, up to 98 percent of crimes are not prosecuted by authorities,
and a common saying is that "life is worth nothing in Guatemala."[31] The
country's government officials admit, as former president Álvaro Colom
did in 2011, that heavily armed and dangerous drug traffickers "have us
cornered." Attorney General Claudia Paz put it this way: "Guatemala's

state is a very weak state. It doesn't have the resources to face problems as grave as that of narco-trafficking. For traffickers to move down here was very easy because there are some areas of the country where practically there is no presence of the state." When the Mexican drug cartel Los Zetas comes into the remote northern areas of Guatemala, "they offer 'plata o plomo, money or bullets.' In essence they say to farmers whose land they want 'You can sell to us and leave this area walking, or you can refuse and you will be carried out of here feet first.'"[32]

Guatemala is located in the middle of the smuggling route between Colombia and the United States, which makes it a convenient transshipment point for drugs coming up from South America. Poor, mostly indigenous farmers in countries like Colombia, Peru, Bolivia, and Ecuador—who themselves have been crushed by economic globalization—have turned to cultivating coca plants, from which the narcotic drug cocaine is derived. This lucrative crop is grown, processed into powdered cocaine, run north, and sold in the United States and Canada where there is always an insatiable demand. But because drug addiction and abuse ruins people's lives, the United States has tried in vain to eradicate cocaine at the source by spending as much as a trillion dollars since the 1970s on the so-called drug war in Latin America.[33] Of course, cocaine production has not decreased, addiction in the north has continued, and the war on drugs has failed.[34]

The appalling criminality associated with the drug trade in Latin America would be diminished, or perhaps not even exist, were there not such an overwhelming demand and willingness to pay large sums of cash for narcotics. In 2010 Americans spent an estimated 28 billion dollars on cocaine alone, which amounted to 150 pure metric tons of the drug.[35] The result in Latin America has been grisly violence, shameless corruption, and narco-terrorism, as drug gangs and the mafia have killed and displaced millions of people in their fight to monopolize the nefarious trafficking business. On top of it all, the vast majority of the money gained from drug sales—variously referred to as "blood dollars" and "the proceeds of murder and misery"—is laundered and safely stashed away in large multinational banks such as Wachovia and HSBC.[36] Once again, the pattern holds whereby the devastating costs are externalized while the vast profits flow northward.

Even Otto Pérez Molina, the corrupt president of Guatemala who as an army commander going by the name Major Tito slaughtered thousands of indigenous Guatemalans while on the U.S. CIA's payroll in the 1980s, can now see that both the Cold War and the drug war have drained his country of resources that should have been spent on more constructive activities. In a candid 2014 commentary, he wrote the following: "If the money and weapons invested in both wars had been invested in education, health, and jobs, things would look different today. So, yes, there are structural factors that explain long-term trends of migration from Guatemala to the U.S. And, yes, these factors are related to lack of social opportunities and violence."[37] Despite Molina's own looting of Guatemala and conspicuous ownership of estates, planes, yachts, and luxury cars, he claimed—rightly—that what the country most needs today is not a war on drugs, but a war on malnutrition.

In the neighboring countries of El Salvador and Honduras, the situation is strikingly similar. A telling excerpt from a July 2015 interview with former Honduran president Manuel Zelaya illustrates how Honduras has been affected by economic globalization. Asked by *Democracy Now!* journalist Juan González about the American media's fixation on crime and violence and the tens of thousands of Honduran women and children fleeing to the United States, Zelaya responded:

> In this regard, measures of repression have been adopted—that is, closing the borders, militarizing the borders, preventing persons from exercising their right to migrate. Because migrating is a right. It is a human right. All of our countries emerged from migration, the United States itself from European migration. Yet it must be regulated. It must have a legal framework. Instead, you see soldiers simply stopping children who are looking for their mothers in the United States, or young people who are looking for a job, because this capitalist, neoliberal exclusionary and highly exploitive society doesn't offer them opportunities. Recall that these societies are run by large transnational corporations: large transnational banks, large transnational commercial concerns, large transnational oil companies. These are governments of the transnationals.[38]

Democratically elected Zelaya—a friend of Cuba's Raúl Castro and Venezuela's Hugo Chávez—served as president of Honduras from January 2006 before being ousted in a U.S.-backed military coup d'état in June 2009. Although then U.S. secretary of state Hillary Clinton publicly condemned the overthrow of Zelaya, emails released in 2015 indicate the U.S. State Department actually endorsed both the coup and new, unelected, pro-business president Roberto Micheletti.[39]

In 2004, a decade after NAFTA went into effect, the Central American Free Trade Agreement (CAFTA) was signed. In essence, it is an extension of economic globalization into Costa Rica, El Salvador, Guatemala, Honduras, and Nicaragua (the Dominican Republic is also included, although it is located in the Caribbean). As was the case with NAFTA, it pushes for open economic frontiers and neoliberal economic policies like deregulation and privatization, but prohibits the free movement of people. Also like NAFTA, the main results have been massive economic instability, lower wages, environmental destruction, and human displacement. The importation of cheap American grains such as rice and corn, for example, put small Central American farmers out of business because they could not grow or sell their crops as cheaply as large American agribusinesses could. The combination of impoverishment and insecurity in Guatemala, Honduras, and El Salvador allowed organized crime to fill the void, resulting in widespread drug gang violence and migration northward.

Prominent American politicians who pushed hard for NAFTA and CAFTA are, for the most part, comfortably in retirement. George W. Bush, whose administration negotiated CAFTA, is living in a multimillion-dollar mansion in Dallas, Texas. Unwilling to acknowledge the increased poverty and inequality that resulted from his administration's policies, Mr. Bush spends his days watercolor painting, riding his mountain bike, and occasionally giving speeches. One typical talk was on the topic of the "power of freedom" in November 2012 in the Cayman Islands, the notorious tax haven for corporations and the super-rich.[40] Bush's successors and those who are still in office seem willfully ignorant of the wide-ranging negative effects of their trade deals, especially the connection between economic deregulation, impoverishment, displacement, and international migration. Compounding the problem, they are pushing for immigration policies that would militarize the U.S.-Mexico border and some are dreaming of building the equivalent of a Great Wall to stop the population flow. Referring to the surge in the number of unaccompanied children at America's southern border in 2014, President Obama's message to the Central Americans was "do not send your children to the borders. If they do make it, they'll get sent back."[41]

Looking elsewhere in the Global South, we see similar patterns of interference and disruption, economic turmoil, and emigration. Few regions have been as volatile as the Middle East and North Africa, where war has dislocated millions of people and led to mass migration. Just as the United States resists unwanted migration from its southern neighbors, so too does the European Union try to prevent the large-scale migration of millions of refugees from the south and east.

THE MIDDLE EAST: SYRIA

Poverty and security are relative concepts. No matter how chaotic or crowded it may be in Germany, France, Greece, and Italy, the conditions there are safer than in war-ravaged countries such as Afghanistan, Iraq, Libya, and Syria. I was reminded of this on a visit to an asylum seeker shelter in the southwestern German state of Baden-Württemberg, where asylees from the Middle East and Africa were living. They stayed in simple rooms, ate ordinary meals prepared in a communal kitchen, and had a curfew each evening. To the average outside visitor, the relatively cramped quarters and restricted freedom of movement seemed like an unacceptable imposition. But to the people living there who had escaped war, violence, social unrest, abject poverty, and various forms of political oppression, there was at least enough to eat and the surroundings were verdant and peaceful. Regardless of how Spartan conditions in the shelter appeared, it was infinitely better than what they had left behind.

Practically anywhere in Europe is preferable to the Yarmouk refugee camp outside the Syrian capital of Damascus. The camp is about two square kilometers in size and lies only five kilometers south of the ancient city center. The suburb became a massive refugee camp when Israel was founded in 1948 and an estimated 600,000 Palestinians were forced out of their homes and off their land. It is yet another irony of history that European Jews, themselves refugees from the Holocaust and World War II, realized their dream of creating an independent state by displacing hundreds of thousands of Arabs. Most Palestinians resettled in the surrounding countries of Lebanon, Syria, Jordan, and Egypt. Over time Yarmouk became a massive refugee city with bustling cafés, restaurants, hair salons, auto shops, and other businesses. At its height, 160,000 Palestinians lived there and it was known as the unofficial capital of the Palestinian Diaspora.

Following the outbreak of the Syrian civil war in March 2011, the troubles of the Palestinian refugees in Yarmouk worsened as opposing militias fought for control of the country. Because some people supported the Free Syrian Army, which was trying to overthrow ruthless Syrian dictator Bashar Assad, Assad's military mercilessly bombarded the camp. In April 2015, Islamic State militants took control of Yarmouk and brutalized approximately 18,000 refugees who remained trapped without food, clean water, or medicine. According to the United Nations Relief and Works Agency for Palestine Refugees (UNRWA), people in the camp were reduced to eating only 400 calories per day (an average daily diet is based on about 2,000 calories). The UN agency's spokesman, Christopher Gunness, painted a dire picture: "The situation in Yarmouk is beyond inhumane. The camp has descended into levels of inhumanity which are unknown even in Yarmouk, and this was a society in which women died in childbirth for lack of medicine, and children died of malnutrition."[42] After 2,000 people escaped from the camp, which resembled a post-apocalyptic war zone, the Islamic State militia sealed off the area and would not let anyone leave or enter. Even international aid organizations such as the United Nations and Save the Children were prevented from entering to help malnourished and injured refugees, including some 3,500 children.

The situation in war-torn Syria as a whole is best described as "beyond inhumane." The country has suffered years of civil war that destroyed its infrastructure and reduced its cities to rubble. The United Nations High Commissioner for Refugees (UNHCR) noted in September 2015 that the value of the Syrian pound had dropped 90 percent since the war began, electricity was available only a couple hours a day at best, and water was scarce. Out of a total population of 22 million, eight million Syrians were internally displaced and four million lived as refugees in neighboring countries: 1.94 million were registered in Turkey; 1.11 million in Lebanon; 629,266 in Jordan, 249,463 in Iraq; 132,375 in Egypt.[43] There are many more unregistered refugees as well, which means the real totals are certainly higher. A Syrian woman from Damascus who fled to Jordan, where she and her husband and three children lived in a storage unit, said she felt imprisoned by the situation: "We don't go out, we don't do anything . . . We have lost any hope we had left for our future."[44] Another man from Aleppo who fled to Jordan with his wife and ten children said, "we have already borrowed

3,000 JOD (US$4,230) just to pay the rent. We haven't eaten any meat for two months."[45] Dreadful as it sounds, they were the lucky ones who made it out alive.

The United Nations estimates that at least 250,000 Syrians have died since the civil war began in 2011, while the Syrian Observatory for Human Rights puts the number at 260,000 (both are conservative underestimates—the real total may be closer to 470,000).[46] Of all the victims of the conflict, none captured the world's attention more than three-year-old Aylan Kurdi. On September 2, 2015, his lifeless body washed ashore near the Turkish resort town of Bodrum after the small rubber dinghy he and his family were riding in capsized in the Mediterranean. He lay facedown in the sand wearing a little red T-shirt, blue trousers, and tiny shoes as waves washed up around him on the beach. Hundreds of thousands of people had died and countless stories were told about the humanitarian tragedy unfolding in Syria over the years, but the death of this one innocent child was different. It humanized the suffering and death in one stark, simple, heartbreaking image.

The Kurdi family was trying to reach the Greek island of Kos, a mere three miles away from the Turkish coast. Originally from Kobani, Syria, they had fled the war and were living as refugees in Istanbul, Turkey. The father of the family, Abdullah Kurdi, had tried to emigrate with his family to Vancouver, Canada, where his sister lives, but lacked the proper travel documents. Out of desperation he reportedly paid 4,000 euros (given to him by his sister) for the fatal boat ride that would have delivered them to Greece. From there they could have made their way north, perhaps to Austria, Germany, or Sweden. Instead, their unseaworthy dinghy capsized after embarking at three in the morning, killing Mr. Kurdi's wife and two young sons along with approximately ten others. A devastated Mr. Kurdi told reporters the next day after claiming their bodies at a Turkish morgue, "now I don't want anything . . . what was precious is gone. What I really want now is for the smuggling to stop, and to find a solution for those people who are paying the blood of their hearts just to leave."[47]

As the number of registered Syrian refugees rose from 10,000 at the beginning of 2012 to more than two million in 2013, three million in 2014, and four million in 2015, so too did the number trying to reach Europe.[48] One common route to Europe is by sea to Greece, which the Kurdi family was attempting to take, and another is by land to Bulgaria.

Greece and Bulgaria are two of the poorest members of the European Union, and neither is particularly welcoming of migrants. Those who enter are encouraged to move on to more generous and welcoming northern European countries like Germany and Sweden—and that is precisely what they do. German interior minister Thomas de Maizière announced in August 2015 "we've got to reckon there will be 800,000 people coming to Germany as refugees or seeking asylum. It will be the largest influx in the country's post-war history. It's a challenge for all of us at the state, federal and local levels. We can master this challenge. I don't think this will overwhelm Germany. We can handle this."[49] Not long after the German Interior Minister made this unflinching statement, the expected number of asylum seekers was revised upward to one million.[50] Immigration rose unmistakably from its normal "low politics" status to "high politics"—that is, one of the most important topics on both Germany and Europe's political agenda.

The causes of the crushing global refugee crisis are complex, indeed, but the root of the conflict in Syria traces back to the Arab Spring and the devastating war in neighboring Iraq that destabilized the region. Few politicians from the major European or American political parties seem capable of connecting the dots between the war profiteering of the military industrial complex, the wars in the Middle East, and the millions of traumatized refugees. Even fewer are willing to take any responsibility for the humanitarian disaster or admit culpability for war crimes. But there are occasionally some who step forward courageously and speak truth to power, such as German Left Party parliamentarian Annette Groth, who said unequivocally that "it is war, it is terror, and it is the former U.S. government who is accountable for it, and the NATO state governments. I'm very sorry to say so, but it is the truth. It was Bush who invaded Iraq."[51] In a rare candid moment in March 2015, U.S. president Barack Obama acknowledged as much, saying that the Islamic State terrorist group "is a direct outgrowth of al-Qaeda in Iraq that grew out of our invasion. Which is an example of unintended consequences. Which is why we should generally aim before we shoot."[52] This admission came too late for the millions of people killed, maimed, orphaned, and displaced by the wars in Afghanistan, Iraq, and Syria—whom the U.S. military considers "collateral damage." From a world-systems perspective, these wars are what capitalist countries do in order to protect their investments abroad and to gain access to oil and other natural resources. Predictably, people displaced by the conflicts flee to wherever they can find safety, often migrating back to core countries.[53] Without a doubt, it is the most troubling and tragic form of global migration.

NORTH AFRICA: LIBYA

Libyan dictator Muammar Gaddafi was known for his bizarre behavior and strange stunts. In August 2010 he made a two-day visit to Italy, Libya's former colonial ruler. On the first day he gave an hour-long talk to a group of two hundred female models, all paid to sit patiently in attendance and listen, in which he advised Europeans to convert to Islam, passed out copies of the Koran, and explained how great women's rights are in Libya. On the second day, with Italian prime minister Silvio Berlusconi at his side, he gave a speech that caught the attention of observers around the world. Here is a condensed sampling of what the unconventional dictator said to his Roman audience:

> Italy needs to convince her European allies to accept this Libyan proposal: five billion euros to Libya to stop illegal immigration. Europe runs the risk of turning black from illegal immigration, it could turn into Africa. We need support from the European Union to stop this army trying to get across from Libya, which is their entry point. At the moment there is a dangerous level of immigration from Africa into Europe and we don't know what will happen. What will be the reaction of the white Christian Europeans to this mass of hungry uneducated Africans? We don't know if Europe will remain an advanced and cohesive continent or if it will be destroyed by this barbarian invasion. We have to imagine that this could happen but before it does we need to work together.[54]

Psychologists studying international migration are invited to go to school on this brief, outlandish excerpt. Needless to say, it was dismissed across Europe as an absurd form of blackmail, but there was more to the indecent proposal than at first meets the eye. Two years prior, both countries had signed a "Friendship Treaty" whereby Italy returned migrants rescued at sea directly to Libya, which kept the number reaching Italian shores very low. On the one hand, Gaddafi was just bluntly stating the facts: Libya needs help from Europe; it is indeed a transit country for Africans on their way north; the future is uncertain and, yes, both countries need to cooperate. On the other hand, he was playing on the fear and racism found in every country in Europe. He was putting into words what many average people hesitate to say publicly for fear of being branded a hateful bigot or neofascist, namely that impoverished African immigrants resemble an invasion that threatens to irrevocably alter European society.

With the cooperation of Gaddafi under the Friendship Treaty, the number of migrants caught entering Italy illegally had dropped from 32,052 in 2008 to 7,300 in 2009.[55] Yet when revolution swept through North Africa and the Middle East in 2011, the situation in Libya grew increasingly chaotic and everything changed. Muammar Gaddafi, the Western-backed dictator of forty-two years, was overthrown with the help of NATO military airstrikes. Much like the ignominious end of Saddam Hussein in Iraq, he was caught hiding in a drainpipe and brutally beaten to death by rebel Misrata militiamen yelling "Allahu Akbar!"[56] Libya descended into the abyss of a bloody civil war and the number of refugees fleeing to the peaceful shores of Italy and other European countries skyrocketed. In 2013, 42,925 migrants and asylum seekers arrived in Italy, and in 2014 that number quadrupled to 170,100. Federico Soda, chief of the International Organization for Migration in Italy, explained that "these figures suggest that the flows are linked to the deteriorating multiple and complex humanitarian crises near Europe's external borders, including the war in Syria and the unrest caused by the political instability in Libya. Many of these people are fleeing war, persecution and totalitarian regimes."[57] Many also saw the central Mediterranean route through Libya to Europe as their only escape.

Those arriving in Libya with the goal of boarding ships to take them to Italy and Malta tell harrowing stories. Sekou Balde, a twenty-year-old migrant who traveled through Libya en route to Lampedusa, Italy, described his experience when Libyan soldiers assaulted him and a group of fellow African migrants: "They said 'where is your money?' I said I didn't have any. Then they attacked me. It was four of them against me. They came to where we were living at one in the morning. My brother was shot dead in front of me—boom, boom—as well as two of my friends."[58] Other migrants who survived the passage through Libya described similar abuse at the hands of human smugglers. "The Libyans take you, they say 'we will shoot you in the head if you don't give us all the money," said a twenty-three-year-old Somali named Mohamud

Cabdale Cali, "sometimes they gave us no food for three days. Then you get a single piece of bread. They kept us in a big house. There were over 200 people—Somalis, Sudanese, Eritreans—but only one toilet. We slept on mats on the floor."[59] One smuggler ferrying people to Europe said warring militias had made conditions in Libya so dangerous that "the Africans are seeing death in front of their eyes," yet "even if there is a 99 percent chance that they are going to die at sea, they are still going to do it because they are just fed up."[60]

To a certain extent, the flight of so many people is beyond description and understanding. Words and theories fail to capture what is really going on in the hearts and minds of human beings. It conjures up, for lack of a more fitting explanation, images of predator and prey in nature: When a gazelle is being chased in the wild by a lion and is about to be caught, it will occasionally spring into a lake or pond. This is usually a last, frantic act to avoid certain death, because the lion (and inevitably hyenas) will simply wait at the shore for the gazelle to lose its strength and drown in the water. I risk this analogy, flawed as it is, only to point out that the exodus of forced migrants from North Africa and the Middle East into the Mediterranean Sea is a final act of desperation. Refugees know the great peril of trying to cross the water to Europe, but what other choice do they have? It is in many cases a tragic attempt to escape the beasts of starvation and war.

SOUTH ASIA: CAPITALISM VERSUS THE CLIMATE IN BANGLADESH

Climate change and environmental disasters hit poor countries hardest of all. Displacement is already occurring in vulnerable regions and it looks likely that changes in the global environment will force more people to migrate in the coming decades. The scientific evidence behind global warming is clear and unmistakable, and we have known for years what the consequences will be if nothing is done. As *National Geographic* reported in a September 2004 special edition, this is what happens when average global temperatures increase:

> Carbon dioxide levels rise. Mercury climbs. Oceans warm. Glaciers melt. Sea level rises. Sea ice thins. Permafrost thaws. Wildfires increase. Lakes shrink. Lakes freeze up later. Ice shelves collapse. Droughts lin-

ger. Precipitation increases. Mountain streams run dry. Winter loses its bite. Spring arrives earlier. Autumn comes later. Plants flower sooner. Migration times vary. Habitats change. Birds nest earlier. Diseases spread. Coral reefs bleach. Snowpacks decline. Exotic species invade. Amphibians disappear. Coastlines erode. Cloud forests dry. Temperatures spike at high altitudes.[61]

These profound effects of global warming are expected to slam the countries of the Global South. Add poverty, high birthrates, and armed conflict to the unfolding climate crisis and the likely result will be an increase in transnational migration.

The worsening predicament has been addressed in such books as Jared Diamond's *Collapse: How Societies Choose to Fail or Succeed* (2006) and Naomi Klein's *This Changes Everything: Capitalism vs. The Climate* (2014). The titles of both capture the grave dilemma the world is facing—either make the collective decision to rein in turbo-capitalism or watch our interconnected societies fail along with the global ecology. Klein rightly argues that we have not lowered carbon emissions because doing so fundamentally conflicts with economic globalization and the logic of deregulated capitalism: "We are stuck because the actions that would give us the best chance of averting catastrophe—and would benefit the vast majority—are extremely threatening to an elite minority that has a stranglehold over our economy, our political processes, and most of our media outlets."[62] This insightful commentary is in line with Jared Diamond's earlier warning that we are on an unsustainable course toward global societal collapse. Our collective demographic, societal, and environmental problems, he says, "are like time bombs with fuses of less than 50 years."[63]

No country in the world will be spared the effects of global climate change, but some regions of the Global South will likely suffer more than others. In Asia, glaciers in the Himalayas are disappearing. This is problematic because they play a vital role in the ecosystem and hold vast amounts of ice that, when it melts, flows into Asia's largest rivers. The Indus, Ganges, Yangtze, and Yellow Rivers all begin in the Himalaya Mountains and supply nearly 1.5 billion people in the densely populated areas of South and East Asia—for example, China, India, Pakistan, and Bangladesh—with water. Among these countries, all of which will undoubtedly be affected by global climate change, Bangladesh is arguably the most vulnerable. With a population of 169 million squeezed into an area smaller than the U.S. state of Iowa, it is one of the most densely populated countries in the world. It is also among the poorest, with half the population working in agriculture and many others in industrial textile factories producing cheap garments for export.[64]

Bangladesh borders India and Myanmar, and its main geographic feature is the Ganges Delta—the largest estuary in the world—where the Ganges and Brahmaputra Rivers converge and empty into the Bay of Bengal. Viewed from space, satellite images of the area show a spectacular mélange of more than two hundred rivers running vein-like through southern Bangladesh, curving and wending in a thousand different ways before emptying brown silt and freshwater from the Himalaya Mountains into the ocean. The view at ground level reveals large areas of the Delta rising just barely a few feet above the water. To be sure, this low-lying land has flooded regularly for the last thousand years, so it is not an unusual occurrence when water surging inland submerges villages during the June to October monsoon season. Cyclones—massive hurricane-strength storms—also hit Bangladesh on a regular basis, sometimes killing hundreds of thousands of people. Cyclone Bhola, for instance, killed between 300,000 and 500,000 people in November 1970, and in 1991 a powerful category 5 cyclone killed 138,000.[65] Warning and shelter systems have improved vastly since then so that far fewer people die when cyclones hit today, but storms around the world are becoming increasingly powerful and frightening. Tropical Cyclone Mahasen displaced 1.1 million Bangladeshis in May 2013, but that paled in comparison to the 4.1 million people displaced in the Philippines by Typhoon Haiyan in November of the same year. Since half of the Bangladeshi population lives within 60 miles of the coast, the potential for future mass climate-related migration is enormous. It is not a question of if but rather when the next super storm will appear.

For the 125 million mostly impoverished Bangladeshis who live in the Ganges-Brahmaputra Delta, extreme weather is a matter of life and death. Some residents give apocalyptic answers to questions about their future. One man said "the sea has been coming closer and closer. God only knows what will happen. Everything will come to an end."[66] Echoing this sentiment, a Delta fisherman stated "we can't do anything else, which is why we think twice about migrating from here. We know the end is coming, but what work will we find to feed our families elsewhere?"[67] Even the country's ambassador to India, Tariq Karim, seems

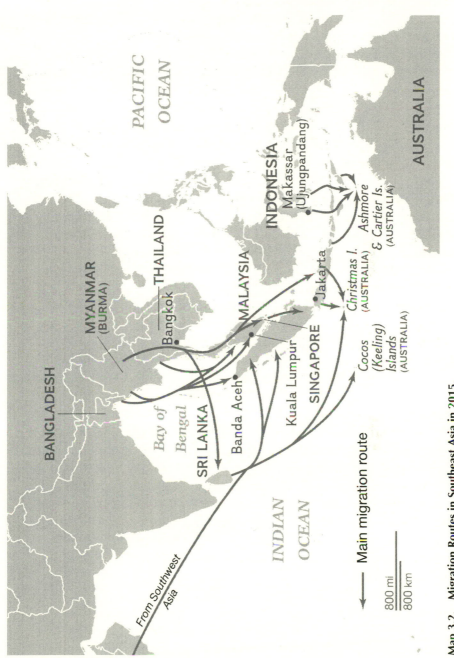

Map 3.2. Migration Routes in Southeast Asia in 2015.

Sources: National Geographic, http://news.nationalgeographic.com/2015/09/150919-data-points-refugees-migrants-maps-human-migrations-syria-world/ (accessed 12 March 2016); Missing Migrants Project, International Organization for Migration.

resigned to what lies ahead. In 2014 he admitted "there is no doubt that preparations within Bangladesh have been utterly inadequate, but any such preparations are bound to fail because the problem is far too big for any single government."[68] Regarding global climate change and his country's vulnerability, he said "we need a regional and, better yet, a global solution. And if we don't get one soon, the Bangladeshi people will soon become the world's problem, because we will not be able to keep them."[69] Precisely what the regional and global solutions will need to entail has been a prominent subject at international climate change conferences in recent years.

At the United Nations Conference of the Parties (COP) negotiations, it is usually poor countries threatened by climate change that argue rich countries should compensate them for loss and damage, while rich countries are loath to discuss the topic of compensation. Countries like Bangladesh point to the fact that industrialized countries have been polluting heavily since the Industrial Revolution began in the eighteenth century and thus are most responsible for global warming. Bangladeshis pollute very little compared to China, India, the United States, or the members of the European Union, yet they are the ones who stand to suffer most from human-caused climate change. Despite their comparatively small carbon footprint, Bangladeshis living in the Ganges Delta could see their simple bamboo huts inundated and forever washed away as the ocean rises in front of them. They are already seeing their drinking water polluted and farmland ruined by salty ocean water. Freshwater fish are also disappearing and waterborne diseases are becoming more common. Bangladesh's leading climate scientist, Atiq Rahman, believes "it's a matter of global justice. These migrants should have the right to move to the countries from which all these greenhouse gases are coming. Millions should be able to go to the United States."[70] In other words, rich countries should not only reduce their carbon emissions, but help pay for the environmental damage they have caused and open their borders to environmental migrants.

BRAIN DRAIN

Brain drain occurs when highly educated people emigrate and their country of origin loses or is drained, so to say, of its most talented and skilled citizens. Such migrants are usually those with university degrees, or who have a particular set of skills, expertise, or specialized knowledge. Information technology specialists, scientists, engineers, teachers, academics, medical doctors, nurses, and healthcare workers figure prominently in this phenomenon. They are part of a distinct type of migration that is associated strongly with the technological revolution involving computers and the Internet that has accompanied twenty-first-century globalization. Brain drain migration flows mostly between core countries (e.g., Europe to North America) or from periphery to core countries (e.g., Africa to Europe), which actively encourage high-skill migrants to immigrate and welcome their arrival.

Skilled migrants leave for a wide range of reasons, but usually because they can earn more money, have greater social opportunities, and enjoy a higher quality of life abroad. The effect on countries that lose such valuable human capital is a serious problem inasmuch as it increases the already large economic disparity between rich and poor. It further disadvantages communities that are already struggling, and it contributes to keeping peripheral countries caught in a cycle of dependency and economic underdevelopment. States that invest resources in educating their citizenry—only to see them leave—lose their investment in people who would otherwise have paid taxes and contributed to the national economy. It has a potentially profound effect on society as well, albeit one that is sometimes hard to pinpoint precisely (it is not always easy to discern when something or someone is gone). According to OECD data, tertiary graduates live longer, earn more, vote more, are more civically engaged, satisfied with their lives, and less violent than nongraduates.[71] Ultimately, it is difficult to replace productive, industrious, highly educated people who possess specialized knowledge. When they disappear, their absence represents a deep loss.

Examples of brain drain abound. An illustrative case is South Africa during the 1990s. When Nelson Mandela was let out of prison in February 1990 and apartheid officially ended with democratic elections in April 1994, the country experienced high levels of social conflict, ethnic tension, and violence. Consequently, there was an exodus of skilled South Africans to Australia, Europe, and North America. Doctors and nurses who had received excellent medical training in apartheid-era South Africa decided there were not only better jobs in places like Ireland, Canada, and New Zealand but also less crime and more opportunities for their families. Yet these were precisely the talented and knowledgeable people the country needed most when the HIV/AIDS pandemic exploded. As demand for health care workers increased dramatically in South Africa, doctors and nurses headed for greener pastures abroad.

CONCLUSION

"The origins of the catastrophe," Karl Polanyi wrote, "lay in the Utopian endeavor of economic liberalism to set up a self-regulating market system."[72] Capitalism, of course, could not regulate itself, which led to colonialism and imperialism and economic underdevelopment. A brutal combination of expropriation of communal land, dislocation, exploitation, and impoverishment initiated and perpetuated international migration. In colonial times it was a foreign imperial master who took land, extracted natural resources, and uprooted people. In neocolonial times it is local elites who collaborate with foreign corporations to enrich themselves at the expense of the working poor. Summing it up, the relationship between the countries of the Global North and South remains economically and politically unequal.

As illustrated in the maquiladoras along Mexico's northern border, multinational corporations (MNCs) set up shops that in some ways resemble the Satanic Mills of nineteenth-century Europe at the height of the Industrial Revolution. The time and place are different, but the degree of alienation and estrangement people feel toward their work is essentially the same. The Mexican minimum wage is about 60 cents an hour—well below the poverty line—and the real profits of companies that do business there flow almost entirely northward. With the help of politicians committed to economic globalization, multinational corporations operate freely in their endless pursuit of profits—regardless of whether their detrimental business practices wreck the environment, sicken the people, or disrupt whole communities. It is little surprise, then, that so many poor people, including children, take dangerous risks riding atop cargo trains in order to reach the United States.

Migration is facilitated by transportation systems originally designed to carry goods along international trade routes. Freight trains and railroads, ships and harbors, planes and airports, buses and highways all increase mobility and allow migrants to pick up and move. In addition, modern communication systems facilitate the process. People in peripheral countries have seen the powerful images on television of life in the rich, northern, industrialized, core countries. But these images are frequently a mirage, because when they arrive in the countries of the Global North they often end up doing dirty, dangerous, demanding minimum-wage jobs that natives are unwilling to do.

To maintain the dominant positions of rich core countries and multinational corporations, and to keep the global economic system from collapsing, core states use the military industrial complex to intervene in peripheral countries—such as Iraq, Afghanistan, and Syria, to name but a few. Since war is bad for the planet and all living things, people inevitably flee as if running out of a house engulfed in flames and seek refuge wherever they can. The result is large numbers of refugees and, increasingly, climate-related migration out of the searing, impoverished countries of the Global South and into the industrialized countries of the Global North.

CHAPTER 4

THE GLOBAL NORTH

"All my life I have been a nomad. I have wandered, rootless. Every place I have settled in, I have been forced to flee; every certainty I have been taught, I have cast aside."[1] So begins Ayaan Hirsi Ali's gripping autobiography *Nomad: A Personal Journey Through the Clash of Civilizations*. The book tells the remarkable story of a young woman who moved from Somalia, her country of birth, to Saudi Arabia, Ethiopia, Kenya, and back again just in time to see her homeland descend into a devastating civil war that killed 350,000 people and displaced half the population. Then, at age twenty-two, her father decided she should marry a distant cousin living in Toronto, Canada, whom she did not know. She was put on a plane and sent off to wed the stranger, but on a stopover in Germany she instead fled by train to the Netherlands, where she applied for political asylum.

In Holland, one of the most egalitarian and livable places in the world, Hirsi Ali mastered the Dutch language and earned a degree in political science from Leiden University. She was motivated by a desire to understand why there was such a difference between stable, prosperous, and democratic Northwestern Europe and the unstable, poor, and corrupt places she had previously known. While studying and working as a translator she came to see how Muslim women in Europe still suffered under the strict patriarchal rules and religious edicts of their immigrant communities. In the process of her intellectual transformation and social awakening, the once pious Muslim girl left Islam and became an atheist. In 2003 she was elected to the lower house of the Dutch parliament as a member of the libertarian Party for Freedom and Democracy, where she began speaking out against radical Islam.

As a parliamentarian, Hirsi Ali raised awareness of female genital mutilation (which she experienced at age five) and so-called "honor killings" in which immigrant women who have supposedly shamed the family are murdered by their male relatives. She criticized the liberal Dutch immigration model that allowed unassimilated ethnic enclaves to form within Dutch society. She also helped Theo van Gogh, a descendent of the famous expressionist painter Vincent van Gogh, make a short, provocative film entitled *Submission*, which exposed the abusive treatment of women in Muslim societies. For his efforts, van Gogh was assassinated in broad daylight on an Amsterdam street. Mohammed Bouyeri, a fanatic twenty-six-year-old Muslim who had immigrated to Holland as a child, shot van Gogh eight times and tried to decapitate him before pinning a note onto his bullet-riddled body. Written on the note was a death threat against Ayaan Hirsi Ali.

Theo van Gogh's death in 2004 propelled Hirsi Ali to international prominence. She was given bodyguards, sent into hiding, and subjected to greater public scrutiny. When Dutch authorities reexamined her original political asylum case from a decade earlier it was revealed that she probably should not have been given asylum in Holland, and she herself admitted she had lied about some of the details of her application. In most cases, lying on an asylum application is grounds for rejection or deportation, but this did not happen to the high-profile politician. While she resigned from parliament, other doors opened up. She moved to the United States in order to work at the right wing American Enterprise Institute and later as a fellow at Harvard University's Kennedy School of Government. As she explains it, "I came to America—like many before me—in search of an opportunity to build a life and a livelihood in freedom and in safety, a life that would be an ocean away from all the strife I had witnessed and the inner conflict I had suffered."[2] She has since gained American citizenship.

Hirsi Ali's candid criticism of Islam and the murder of Theo van Gogh were part of a renewed discussion in the Netherlands and Europe about immigration. In neighboring Denmark the *Jyllands-Posten* newspaper published controversial cartoon images of the Prophet Muhammad that sparked demonstrations across Europe and the Middle East. In France a state of emergency was declared in November 2005 when marginalized immigrant youths rioted against police brutality and racism. In Holland the government began to critically reassess its immigration policies. Even those who had previously been open to immigration wondered whether their politically correct, tolerant, multicultural Dutch Model had failed because it had not pushed Muslims to more fully integrate into society. At Mohammed Bouyeri's murder trial, for instance, he told the court the killing had not been "personal" but that his understanding of Islam compelled him "to chop off the head of anyone who insults Allah and the Prophet."[3] It was hard for some on the left to acknowledge that Holland was struggling with multiculturalism, and that radical Islam was indeed a problem.

EUROPE

The Global North refers to the industrialized, economically developed, wealthy countries of the world. They comprise the core of the capitalist world-system and include most of Europe, the United States, Canada, Australia, New Zealand, and Japan. While core countries hold the lion's share of the world's wealth, they make up about 13 percent of the global population.[4] As noted earlier, two-thirds of global migration involves the countries of the Global North: 40 percent flows from South to North, 22 percent North to North, and 5 percent North to South.[5] These percentages are subject to variation depending on how countries are classified, but they provide a bird's-eye view of worldwide population flows.

Of particular interest here is South to North migration and migration within the North. Why are millions of people moving from peripheral to core countries and, in some cases, risking their lives and literally dying to get there? What does free movement within the European Union say about the dual processes of globalization and migration? To explore these questions, let us turn to Europe, where the capitalist world-system emerged in the sixteenth century and proceeded to spread around the globe. For it is here we see some of the best illustrations of both the benefits and challenges of globalization: the advantages of free movement within the Schengen zone; the dilemma of freedom versus security; capitalism's insatiable demand for cheap labor; the demographic deficit caused by low birthrates; growing pains associated with the transition from homogeneous to multicultural societies; the difficulties of integrating and assimilating immigrant "others;" and the attempt to maintain national sovereignty in an age of open frontiers.

BRITAIN

The British Empire played a significant role in the expansion of the global capitalist market. As the saying goes, the sun never set on the British Empire, which at its peak in the early twentieth century stretched around the world from the Americas to Africa and Asia and included one-quarter of the world's landmass. The relationship between Britain and its colonies exemplified, in quintessential fashion, how core countries exploited peripheral countries; how the colonies supplied natural resources that were exported back to the mother country; how colonies in Africa, Asia, and the Americas remained underdeveloped as a result. With regard to international migration, people moved in both directions—from the core to the periphery and back. At first, European administrators, settlers, businessmen, and the like moved to the colonies. Over time, residents of the colonies migrated back to the seat of the empire. Indians, Pakistanis, Nigerians, Kenyans, and Jamaicans, for instance, all migrated to Great Britain because of the administrative, linguistic, economic, and political ties between the core and periphery.

Following World War II, Britain (like Germany and France and others) needed labor during the postwar economic recovery. To meet this need, large numbers of Irish immigrated to Britain. In addition, workers from India, Pakistan, and the Caribbean came in the 1950s and early 1960s during a time when migrating was relatively easy. The 1948 British Nationality Act gave citizens of the New Commonwealth (i.e., the newly independent former colonies) the unrestricted right to enter and live in the country. This changed, however, with the 1962 Commonwealth Immigrants Act, which put restrictions on entry and began to more tightly control nonwhite immigration. More restrictive legislation followed in 1968 and 1971 in an attempt to keep out people from the former colonies who did not have strong ties (such as a British parent or grandparent) to the United Kingdom.

Conservative politicians such as Enoch Powell advocated stricter controls, a stop to nonwhite immigration, and even repatriation to countries of origin. In his infamous 1968 "Rivers of Blood Speech" he predicted Britain's population would one day be 10 percent nonwhite. "As I look ahead," he said, "I am filled with foreboding; like the Roman, I seem to see 'the River Tiber foaming with much blood.'"[6] He envisioned a nightmare scenario and warned that Britain would soon resemble the United States, which was then experiencing race riots in the wake of Martin Luther King, Jr.'s assassination: "The tragic and intractable phenomenon which we watch with horror on the other side of the Atlantic but which there is interwoven with the history and existence of the States itself, is coming upon us here by our own volition and our own neglect. Indeed, it has all but come. In numerical terms, it will be of American proportions long before the end of the century."[7] Enoch Powell was dismissed in 1968 from his position in the Conservative Party's Shadow Cabinet for his bigoted views. He died in 1998 after having seen the nonwhite immigrant population grow from 50,000 in 1953 to 3.7 million.[8]

Traditionally, Britain has not viewed itself as a "country of immigration"—that is, like Australia, Canada, or the United States, where it is taken for granted that most of the population is of immigrant stock. Yet over time it has become a reluctant country of immigration. For much of the nineteenth and twentieth centuries more people left than entered, and only toward the end of the twentieth century, from 1983 onward, was there a net influx of migrants. It joined the European Community (now Union) in 1973 but not the Schengen Agreement, which allows free movement within the Schengen Area of Europe (a topic we will return to below). A crucial turning point arrived with the fall of the Berlin Wall in November 1989 and the final dissolution of the Soviet Union in 1991. Eastern Europe opened up, the capitalist economic market expanded eastward, and migrants poured out. Many came to Britain, including more than half a million Poles.

Great Britain is an island country and can, at least in theory, protect its borders more easily than continental European countries. Migrants who enter have historically had to come by ship or plane, although since 1994 the 50-kilometer-long underground Channel Tunnel connects Britain and France and one can now enter by train. On the continental French side of the Channel Tunnel, or Chunnel as it is called colloquially, a squalid camp called "the Jungle" has existed for years near the town of Calais. Migrants camp there awaiting an opportunity to make the last leg of their journey across the English Channel. Most attempt to stow away in cargo trucks or shipping containers, or board departing trains and ferries. In the summer of 2015 the chaotic situation reached unprecedented depths as at least nine people died trying to cross through the Chunnel. An estimated 3,000 migrants, many of them refugees from Afghanistan, Iraq, Syria, Eritrea, and Sudan, were camped out in the Jungle and in the town square of Calais waiting for their chance to cross and apply for asylum. As one Syrian put it, "we have breakfast, we smoke, we laugh, we joke, we eat again, and after that in the night we have a try [at escaping to England]. Every night."[9]

FRANCE

Migration to France prior to World War II came largely from within Europe, mostly from countries such as Belgium, Italy, and Poland. Migrants came to fill the demand for labor and were encouraged to settle in France and take French citizenship. After World War II the number of migrants from former colonies in Africa increased, and they too came mostly to fill labor shortages. Just as in Great Britain, the link between colonialism and immigration is clear. Algerians, for instance, migrated in growing numbers after World War II when they were granted French citizenship; by the mid-1950s they were the largest group of African migrants in the country. At first this was considered a type of internal migration, because Algeria was considered an extension of France. When Algeria gained its independence in 1962 nearly 900,000 French-Algerians moved to France. Those who migrated later were considered foreign migrants.

The 1973 Oil Crisis and ensuing global economic recession stopped the organized recruitment of migrant labor. The recession resulted from a chain of events that originated in the Middle East. The United

States and Britain (among others) backed Israel militarily in the 1973 Arab-Israeli War, which the Israelis handily won. In response, the Organization of Arab Petroleum Exporting Countries (OAPEC) began an oil embargo against the West, which caused the price of oil to spike and led to an economic downturn. This put a stop to the importation of guest workers across Northern Europe, but it did not stop the flow of migration in the years that followed. Migrant workers from North Africa stayed in France instead of returning to their homes in Algeria, Morocco, Tunisia, Turkey, and elsewhere, and brought their families to be with them through unification programs.

Underlying the national debate over migration from outside the European cultural sphere, especially Africa, has been concern about preserving French culture and national identity. The official stance is that France is characterized by civic nationalism, as opposed to ethnic nationalism.[10] In other words, once immigrants gain French citizenship, they are French just like everyone else. In practice, however, ethnic nationalism and opposition to immigration remains widespread. The prominence of the right wing National Front and its former leader Jean-Marie Le Pen is a reminder of the continued presence of racism and uneasiness with multiculturalism. Always incendiary, Le Pen said in 1984 that "tomorrow the immigrants will be moving into your house, eating your food and sleeping with your wife, your daughter, your son."[11] His daughter Marine Le Pen assumed leadership of the party in 2011 and distanced herself from her father, but only slightly toned down the rhetoric. She once said Muslims were occupying France (a reference to the Nazi occupation during World War II) and compared the 2015 influx of Middle Eastern war refugees to the fourth-century barbarian invasions of Rome.[12]

GERMANY

In the years after World War II ended in 1945, some twelve million ethnic Germans were expelled from the lost territories east of the Oder-Neisse line (the present border between Germany and Poland). Being ethnic Germans, the expellees had the legal right to settle within the post-war German territories. They also spoke German, so their assimilation into society occurred quickly. The country was split between East and West as well, with the German Democratic Republic (East

Germany) under the control of the Soviet Union and the Federal Republic of Germany (West Germany) associated with the United States and Western Europe. The dynamic between the authoritarian East and democratic capitalist West was shaped in important ways by migration, as the East tried to keep its population from leaving. The East Germans were "voting with their feet" as they showed their dislike of the regime by simply relocating to the West. In order to stop the exodus, East Germany built the Berlin Wall in August 1961, which was an extraordinary case of a wall built to keep people in rather than the more common purpose of keeping them out.

West Germany's rapid economic recovery from the mid-1950s onward, called "the economic miracle," required cheap imported labor. As a result, Germany signed a series of bilateral agreements with Italy, Greece, and Spain to bring in guest workers (the famous *Gastarbeiter*) in order to keep the economy growing. Yet they could not get enough, so they invited more guest workers from countries such as Turkey, Morocco, and Tunisia. The idea was that the workers would be guests and, as the name implies, return home at some point in the future when their services were no longer needed. This did not always happen. Many of the Italians, Greeks, and Spaniards were inclined to return, but guest workers from North Africa had less reason to do so. The Swiss poet Max Frisch captured the essence of the situation with guest workers when he said *"Ein kleines Herrenvolk sieht sich in Gefahr: man hat Arbeitskräfte gerufen, und es kommen Menschen"* (A small master race feels threatened: workers were invited, and human beings are coming).[13] He meant that when people migrate to another country to work, they do other things as well, like start families, raise children, put down roots, and form communities. After a time they prefer to stay rather than return, especially when their country of origin is poor, undemocratic, and economically underdeveloped.

The 1973 Oil Crisis ended the organized recruitment of labor, just as in France, but immigration continued through family reunification programs as guest workers brought their families (usually wives and children) to be with them in Germany. This is largely how the immigrant population grew after World War II, even though Germany did not consider itself to be a "country of immigration" and thus did not readily give citizenship to long-term foreign residents. This gradually changed from 1990 onward, as citizenship policy was liberalized and the country moved away from a strict law of the blood (jus sanguinis) citizenship policy to a conditional law of the soil (jus solis) policy. By 2000 Germany had opened its citizenship policy so that foreign residents could more easily (after eight years of legal residence) acquire citizenship. Like Great Britain, Germany also reluctantly acknowledged, with almost 10 percent of its population foreign born, that it had become a country of immigration.

The long shadow of the Nazis continues to shape modern German politics. In an attempt to atone for crimes committed during World War II, Germany created one of the most liberal asylum laws in the world. Its constitution states (in article 16) that the "politically persecuted enjoy the right to asylum."[14] This generous law was intended to help the politically persecuted, but it became problematic in the 1990s when economic migrants used it to gain entry into the country. Germany did not consider itself to be a "country of immigration" and thus had few legal avenues of entry for foreigners who wanted to migrate, which is why people claimed political asylum. Even if their claim was denied, they were able to enter Germany and oftentimes stay permanently. Since 2004 Germany has implemented a modern immigration law that facilitates the migration and integration of foreigners into the country.[15]

The refugee crisis resulting from the wars in Iraq, Afghanistan, and Syria has profoundly tested Germany. Due to the history of the Holocaust and genocide committed during World War II, many Germans feel ethically obligated to provide refuge to those in need—as a kind of reparation seventy years on. This helps explain why Germany has taken in more refugees and asylum seekers from the Middle East than any other European country since the conflicts there began. Germany's comparatively generous policies have, predictably, acted like a magnet and attracted ever larger numbers of people. With smartphones, social media, and modern communication technology the word spread in 2015 that Germany and other northern countries, especially Sweden, were relatively open to refugees. As a result, hundreds of thousands of Iraqis, Syrians, Afghans, and others set out with the goal of reaching the generous countries of Northern Europe. In September 2015 thousands of people camped out in the Budapest train station waiting to board trains to take them to Vienna and on to Munich. "Germany! Germany!" they chanted in unison, while others held up signs that read "Please, we want to go to Germany."[16]

ITALY

Italy's geographic location makes it a prime destination and logical entry point for migrants coming from Africa and the Middle East. The Italian peninsula extends nearly six hundred miles into the Mediterranean Sea, and the proverbial heel of the Italian boot is a mere 45 miles from Albania. The islands of Sardinia, Sicily, and Lampedusa are 140, 100, and 70 miles, respectively, from the Tunisian coast, and Lampedusa is 184 miles due north of war-torn Libya. In the years following the 2011 Arab Spring, increasing numbers of refugees fleeing civil war in Africa and the Middle East arrived in Italy. In the five-year period from January 2010 to December 2014, a total of 157,140 asylum applications were submitted in Italy, with the annual number increasing from 10,050 in 2010 to 63,660 in 2014.[17] In 2015, the refugee crisis worsened considerably, with approximately 10,000 migrants arriving every month, many of whom embarked from Libya on rickety, overcrowded fishing boats en route to the island of Lampedusa.[18]

A turning point in the recent history of trans-Mediterranean migration to Italy occurred on October 3, 2013, when an estimated 366 people died attempting to reach Lampedusa.[19] More than 500 migrants, mostly from the poor East African countries of Eritrea and Somalia, were crammed into an unseaworthy fishing boat slowly making its way toward Italy's southernmost island. Having drifted for two days in the rough Mediterranean Sea, the trawler got within a half mile of Lampedusa in the dark, early hours of the morning. Someone on the ship attempted to send a distress signal to Italian authorities in Lampedusa by lighting a gas-soaked sheet, which then fell to the floor and started a fire near the fuming engine. In the chaos and mayhem that ensued, the panicked passengers rushed to one side of the boat, causing it to capsize and leaving hundreds of people struggling to stay afloat in the water. While the Italian coast guard allegedly did little to help, local fisherman came to the rescue of 155 people. The rest, including women and children and many who could not swim, drowned within sight of Lampedusa.

The catastrophe repeated itself a week later when dozens of mostly Syrian women and children died at sea under similarly tragic circumstances between the islands of Malta and Lampedusa.[20] In response, the Italian government created a search-and-rescue program called Operation Mare Nostrum, a Latin term dating back to Roman times meaning "Our Sea." The yearlong operation led by the Italian Navy used a combination of frigates, submarines, unmanned drones, helicopters, aircraft with infrared equipment, and a 900-person Marine Brigade team to patrol the Strait of Sicily in order to save the lives of migrants trying to reach Lampedusa. The search-and-rescue mission, which covered a total of 27,000 square miles, was by most accounts a success. In the year that it was implemented, Italian authorities reported that at least 150,810 migrants were rescued at sea and 330 alleged human smugglers "brought to justice."[21]

Regrettably, Mare Nostrum could not save everyone. On September 11, 2014, a boat carrying migrants primarily from Egypt, Syria, Palestine, and Sudan sank off the coast of Malta. The ship's human trafficking captains deliberately scuttled the ship for reasons that are not entirely clear, but probably in order to force Maltese authorities to come to the rescue of the distressed ship. While death counts in such disasters are hard to establish with certainty, it is estimated that 500 people perished. Only eleven survived. Most on board were escaping war and grinding poverty in their home countries and had paid up to $4,000 for the ride. An Egyptian mother of three and wife of one of the missing passengers reported that her Syrian husband "fled to escape the violence and destruction in Syria" and that the traffickers told them "it's a safe trip to Europe and will arrive within several days."[22] Not long thereafter, on September 15, 2014, approximately 250 more people died off the coast of Libya in a similar accident.[23]

Despite ongoing deaths at sea, Operation Mare Nostrum was terminated in October 2014. Italy did not want to pay the monthly sum of 9.5 million euros to run the program or the 1.2 billion euros annually it cost to bring asylum seekers to the mainland and care for them.[24] The biggest reason for ending Mare Nostrum, however, was a public sense that desperate migrants from Africa and the Middle East were overwhelming the country. While the operation had brought many thousands of people to safety, the government as well as a majority of the public saw it as encouraging ever more migrants to risk the dangerous journey into the Mediterranean Sea. Why, they reasoned, should Italy provide incentive to human traffickers bringing poor migrants to Europe? Why attract even more destitute asylum seekers from North Africa when Italy already has enough socioeconomic problems? Do extensive search-and-rescue missions not send a signal to would-be migrants that Europeans welcome their arrival? Why should Italy bear such a large share of the burden of patrolling the Mediterranean when it ought to be a collective European responsibility?

The task of protecting the European Union's southern borders was thus left to the European Agency for the Management of Operational Cooperation at the External Borders of the Member States of the European Union (EU), also known as Frontex. Starting in November 2014 it began an operation code-named Triton, which, compared to Mare Nostrum, was smaller and relatively limited in scope. Whereas Mare Nostrum had patrolled a massive area of the Mediterranean Sea amounting to three times the size of the island of Sicily, Operation Triton extended its surveillance only 30 miles off the Italian coast, used fewer aircraft and ships, and employed sixty-five personnel. The total cost was 2.9 million euros per month, about one-third of what Mare Nostrum had cost. Instead of being a search-and-rescue operation, its primary goal was border control and security. Yet the scaled-back Operation Triton was supported by just twenty-one of the twenty-eight EU member states, and faced opposition from prominent countries like the United Kingdom.

Conservative British prime minister David Cameron's government explained its position in straightforward terms. Asked in October 2014 what contribution Her Majesty's Government would make "to prevent refugees and migrants drowning in the Mediterranean," the Foreign Office responded in writing that "we do not support planned search-and-rescue operations in the Mediterranean. We believe that they create an unintended 'pull factor', encouraging more migrants to attempt the dangerous sea crossing and thereby leading to more tragic and unnecessary deaths."[25] The government also believed "the most effective way to prevent refugees and migrants attempting this dangerous crossing is to focus our attention on countries of origin and transit, as well as taking steps to fight the people smugglers who willfully put lives at risk by packing migrants into unseaworthy boats."[26] Human rights organizations protested this position and warned prophetically of the potential deadly consequences. Maurice Wren, head of the British Refugee Council, cautioned that the "people fleeing atrocities will not stop coming if we stop throwing them life-rings; boarding a rickety boat in Libya will remain a seemingly rational decision if you're running for your life and your country is in flames. The only outcome of withdrawing help will be to witness more people needlessly and shamefully dying on Europe's doorstep."[27] The UNHCR echoed this sentiment and called for a Europe-wide commitment to saving lives in the Mediterranean Sea, stating that "the collective response needs to maintain a strong capacity to rescue people at sea and increase safer ways for refugees to find safety in Europe. If Europe fails in these efforts, many more lives will continue to be lost, and incidents such as the disasters off Lampedusa" will increase in number.[28]

As predicted, refugee boat deaths continued with alarming regularity. In February 2015 approximately 300 mostly African migrants died when their rubber dinghies capsized off the Libyan coast.[29] On April 12, 2015, 400 people died trying to sail from Libya to Lampedusa.[30] A week later, in the biggest refugee shipwreck in the Mediterranean Sea on record, an estimated 800 migrants perished seventeen miles off the Libyan coast.[31] Passengers reportedly rushed to one side of the overcrowded boat in an attempt to flag down a passing ship, causing it to capsize. The Italian coast guard rescued twenty-eight exhausted people and delivered them to Catania, Sicily, but the exact number who died in the shipwreck will likely never be known. Many people are kept in the hull of the vessel, and when the ship goes down they have almost no chance of surviving. On such hazardous voyages there is no official passenger list, and bodies are inevitably lost at sea. According to the UNHCR, approximately 350 Eritreans were on board, along with others from Ethiopia, Gambia, Ivory Coast, Mali, Senegal, Sierra Leone, Somalia, and Syria.[32]

The staggering loss of life in the Mediterranean in the spring of 2015 compelled the European Union to triple the monthly funding for Operation Triton from 2.9 to 9 million euros. The European Commission also presented a "European Agenda on Migration" that pledged to step up efforts to save lives and stem the tide of migration across the Mediterranean. The ambitious agenda was comprised of four pillars: (1) reduce incentives drawing migrants to Europe, address the root causes of forced migration, and crack down on human traffickers, (2) increase external border security, (3) improve measures to effectively handle record numbers of asylum applications, and (4) provide legal pathways to Europe for the mutual benefit of both sending and receiving countries.[33] In announcing the new plan, political leaders struck appropriate notes of sympathy and solidarity. European Commission vice president Frans Timmermans acknowledged that "the loss of life in the Mediterranean has shocked all Europeans."[34] European Union Foreign Affairs representative Federica Mogherini stated that migration across the Mediterranean was "not only a European but a global challenge" and pointed out succinctly that "a real, long term response will come only from fixing the root causes; from poverty to instability caused by wars, to the crises in Libya and Syria."[35]

European Union officials mostly said the right things, but the enormity of the humanitarian crisis they faced was obvious. The 2015 Agenda on Migration had a "mission impossible" aspect to it, for such plans are more readily written than implemented. Fixing the root causes of forced migration is easier said than done. Were eradicating poverty in Africa simple, it would have been done long ago. Ending armed conflict is hard when there is a flourishing international arms trade combined with lots of men with guns who believe war is the answer. On top of it all, economic hardship limits the amount of resources European countries are willing to devote to immigrants when there is already so much need among their own citizens. This is especially the case when a country is heavily indebted and on the brink of bankruptcy.

GREECE

For much of the twentieth century, Greece was a country of emigration rather than immigration, meaning that more people departed than entered. In the decades following World War II, specifically from the early 1950s until the mid-1970s, one million Greeks left the country. Some 600,000 went to the Federal Republic of Germany alone after the two countries signed a guest worker agreement that allowed Greeks to emigrate and help the so-called German *Wirtschaftswunder,* or economic miracle. But over time, the tides of migration turned. About half the Greeks who had left in the decades after World War II returned. Greece became the twelfth member of the European Union in 1981, and when it signed the Schengen Agreement in 2000 it came under pressure to protect its external borders.

Controlling Greece's long borders, however, is exceedingly difficult. A nearly 700-mile land border with Albania, Macedonia, Bulgaria, and Turkey, as well as 8,500 miles of coastline along thousands of islands in the Aegean, Ionian, and Mediterranean Seas, makes trying to regulate who enters the country a seemingly Sisyphean task. Due to Greece's geographic proximity to war-ravaged countries like Syria and Iraq, it is a gateway and transit point for migrants hoping to pass through to the wealthy countries of northwestern Europe. Most who enter Greece move on as soon as possible, but many are also detained there or lack the means to keep going. It is unclear exactly how many undocumented migrants are in Greece, because (by definition) they are hard to track and count. Census data show that in 2011 there were 447,658 registered foreign-born residents out of a total population of 10.8 million; but the actual number of foreign born (including unregistered migrants and refugees) is probably between one and 1.3 million.[36]

The European Court of Justice found that "in 2010 Greece was the point of entry in the European Union of almost 90% of illegal immigrants, resulting in a disproportionate burden being borne by that State compared to other Member States and the inability of the Greek authorities to cope with the situation in practice."[37] In response to this telling statistic, Greece tried to crack down on irregular migration in 2012 by building an eight-mile fence along its border with Turkey. It also implemented "Operation Xenios Zeus," which detained migrants who had illegally entered the country for up to eighteen months in overcrowded, dirty, and dangerous detention centers. The Amygdaleza detention center in Athens, for instance, was described by independent observers as inadequate, lacking medical care, and unhygienic: "It was really the image of a concentration camp," said Nikitas Kanakis of the group Médicins du Monde, who inspected the facility and found migrants "neglected, malnourished and living in isolation without even knowing what the future held for them."[38] In another camp in Komotini near the Turkish border, an aid worker reported "I did not think that such conditions were possible on European soil. The main complaint of migrants is that they are not being treated like human beings, that they are being subjected to a living hell."[39] One man who had been locked up for seven months told the human rights organization Doctors Without Borders that Komotini was filthy beyond words and unfit for animals, let alone humans. "The toilets are not working. The piping system is broken. Excrement is falling from the toilets on the first floor to the ground floor. People are locked up inside almost all day. We are allowed in the yard one hour in the morning and one hour in the evening. And not always every day."[40]

Any attempt to explain how and why the Greek treatment of foreigners got so bad must take into account the fact that the economic crisis of 2008, also referred to as the Great Recession, wreaked havoc on the country. The official unemployment rate practically tripled from 9.6 percent in 2009 to 27.3 percent in 2013, and surpassed 50 percent among young people under twenty-five years of age.[41] The suicide rate, to cite one heart-wrenching study by *The British Medical Journal*, increased by 35.7 percent and hit a thirty-year high in 2012. "The passage of new austerity measures in June 2011," the *BMJ* concluded, "marked the beginning of significant, abrupt and sustained increases in total suicides."[42] During this dark night of the soul in which Greek citizens cut back, went without, slipped into poverty, and struggled for their very survival, the needs of migrants who entered the country illegally were low on the government's list of public policy priorities. Former Greek prime minister Antonis Samaras articulated his New Democratic Party's position in 2014 when he said "we have 1 million unemployed. Should we accept a million illegal immigrants? Should we open the way for more to come? This party will never allow this to happen."[43]

Greece's total debt of 319 billion euros equaled 175 percent of its Gross Domestic Product (GDP) in 2013.[44] It was relying on yet more loans from the European Union and International Monetary Fund to pay back its crippling debt when national elections in the fall of 2014 brought a new coalition government to power. Finance minister Yanis Varoufakis attracted an international following for his unconventional behavior—not wearing a necktie or tucking in his shirt at meetings with stiff EU bureaucrats; riding his black 1300 CC Yamaha motorcycle to work instead of being chauffeured to parliament in a government-provided limousine; flipping the bird to German politicians, and so on—but it was defense minister Panos Kammenos who made extraordinary headlines regarding international migration. Amid speculation that Greece would exit the Euro zone (the so-called "Grexit") and blaming the Germans for forcing fiscal austerity on the already financially strapped Greeks, Kammenos said "if Europe leaves us in the crisis, we will flood it with migrants, and it will be even worse for Berlin if in that wave of millions of economic migrants there will be some jihadists of the Islamic State too."[45] Although the government's deputy immigration minister backed away from the defense minister's position, it was enough to raise eyebrows and sound the alarm bells in the rest of Europe.

Defense Minister Kammenos's threat became a reality in the fall of 2015, when hundreds of thousands of asylum seekers passed through Greece en route to Germany and other Western European countries. Of course, it turned out to be Paris rather than Berlin that was first attacked by Jihadists. Two of the terrorists who participated in the November attacks in the French capital that killed 130 people had, in fact, been fingerprinted in Greece only a month earlier. Posing as asylum seekers, they mixed in with the other migrants and made their way to Paris with the goal of exacting a measure of bloody revenge for France's participation, by way of deadly airstrikes against presumed Islamic State militants, in the Syrian civil war.

SPAIN

At first glance, the enclaves of Ceuta and Melilla appear to be part of Morocco, but in fact they have been under Spanish control for nearly five centuries. The two outposts are particularly noteworthy because they symbolically represent the long history of European colonialism and expansion of the world-economy into Africa. They are the only land borders between Europe and Africa, and, like powerful magnets, attract thousands of migrants every year from countries throughout Africa, the Middle East, and as far away as East Asia.

Ceuta is a small port city with a population of 86,000 and a territory of approximately seven square miles lying at the northwestern tip of the African continent. It is just nine miles south of the mainland Spanish coast, on the southern Strait of Gibraltar where the Mediterranean Sea opens into the Atlantic Ocean. Because of Ceuta's strategic location where two continents come together, it has long had a certain pride of place as an important stop for ships sailing through the Mediterranean, as well as for merchants following overland trading routes between Europe and Africa. Over the centuries many different peoples, including the Phoenicians, Carthaginians, Greeks, Romans, Vandals, Byzantines, Arabs, Portuguese, and Spaniards, have inhabited Ceuta. The Arabs captured the town in 711 CE and from there proceeded to invade the Iberian Peninsula, bringing Islam to Southwestern Europe and changing the course of Spanish history. The Portuguese conquered Ceuta in 1415, making it the first permanent European settlement in Africa. When the Portuguese and Spanish monarchies united in 1580, it became a Spanish commercial trading station and military fort. In the twentieth century Ceuta was known as the place where general Francisco Franco launched his military expedition into mainland Spain at the beginning of the Spanish Civil War in 1936. When Morocco gained its independence from Spain in 1956, however, both Ceuta and Melilla remained in Spanish hands.

The city of Melilla lies 140 miles east of Ceuta. Its nearly 85,000 predominately Roman Catholic inhabitants live on five square miles of land surrounded by Morocco on one side and the Mediterranean Sea on the other. It has belonged to Spain since 1497 and was traditionally a port city, trading post, and military fort. The Moroccans tried many times over the centuries to capture the town, and very nearly managed to when Abd el-Karim laid siege to the city in 1921. A celebration was held in 1997 to commemorate the 500th anniversary of Spanish possession, and today it is an autonomous city that is both a vacation resort for wealthy Europeans and an entry point for migrants into the European Union.

Morocco does not recognize Spain's sovereignty over either Ceuta or Melilla and periodically requests that the cities be returned. Spain refuses and has instead taken a series of measures to strengthen its control over the areas. A crucial turning point came in 1986 when Spain joined the European Community and later became part of the Schengen Area that allows free movement of people within much of the European Union. The Schengen Agreement simultaneously loosened internal border checks and tightened control over external borders, which led to increased measures to secure the perimeters of Ceuta and Melilla. Fences around the enclaves in the early 1990s were ten feet (three meters) high, and then raised to almost twenty feet (six meters). At first there was one fence, then two fences side by side, and finally a row of three fences. Razor wire was hung across the top, infrared cameras were added along with watchtowers, and police patrolled the boundary around the clock with their German shepherd guard dogs.

Ceuta and Melilla became fortresses, and protecting them against people trying to cross illegally from Morocco became a violent business on both sides of the fence. Ample evidence in the form of videos and eyewitness testimony show that Moroccan and Spanish authorities use excessive force against migrants. One of the most lethal cases occurred in February 2014 when Spanish security forces fired rubber bullets and sprayed tear gas at a group of West African migrants who had swum out to sea, around the breakwater, and back into Ceuta. Fifteen, many of whom could only barely tread water, died.[46] Later that year the United Nations High Commissioner for Refugees rebuked Spain when police were photographed using bone-crushing force to stop some 200 migrants from storming the fence at Melilla.[47] In February 2015 Moroccan authorities burned down the shelters where hundreds of migrants were camped at the edge of Melilla. "They burned everything," one migrant said of the Moroccan police, "they hit us on the arms, legs or on the head. I'm hurt too, they've cracked my skull."[48]

It is mostly young African men who arrive at the gates of Ceuta and Melilla, but increasingly the arrivals include women and children. They come mostly from sub-Saharan countries, but also from war-ravaged Middle Eastern countries like Iraq and Syria, and occasionally from as far away as Afghanistan and India. Tens of thousands of people try every year to enter Ceuta and Melilla by land, sea, and air. Most are prevented from getting in, or are forcefully turned away when they try, but approximately 4,200 people penetrated the fortress in 2013.[49] The number of migrants attempting to enter Ceuta and Melilla spiked in 2014, and the most common method of attempted entry was to rush the fence en masse. On May 28, 2014, more than 1,000 people stormed the fence all at once, with about 500 actually reaching the Spanish side.[50] In addition to coordinated attempts, which overwhelm both Moroccan and Spanish police, migrants try to cross into Ceuta and Melilla in a variety of other ways. Some put ladders up against the fence, scale over, and jump onto the Spanish side, while others use boats, swim out to sea, and then back into Spanish territory, stow away in vehicles, or (if they can afford it) are dropped in by helicopter.[51]

Ayuba, a twenty-one-year-old man from the Ivory Coast, left behind his menial farm job in 2003 and began walking toward Ceuta. After crossing Mali, Algeria, and Morocco, he arrived at the Spanish frontier where he camped for sixteen months in the forest before making a desperate attempt in 2005 to enter. He rushed the fence with hundreds of other migrants, five of whom died in the process, and landed on the Spanish side. At the time, he said "I want to work in Europe and send money home," adding that "now everything will get better."[52] It is unclear what became of Ayuba in Europe, but in the decade following his successful crossing, the tide of humanity surging toward the European outposts has grown larger. When migrants arrive they live in squalid camps at the outskirts of town, sometimes for years at a time. The journeys they have behind them are usually marked by extreme hardship, and the stories they tell are replete with various forms of crime and punishment. Some pay exorbitant sums to human traffickers only to be ripped off, or must offer bribes to shamelessly corrupt authorities in the countries they pass through. Others are robbed, assaulted, or raped. Sickness, injury, hunger, and exhaustion are the norm.

The majority of migrants who enter Ceuta and Melilla are returned to Morocco, where most will bide their time and try again to scale the fence. Even if they are stopped at the gates and literally beaten back, most are determined to keep trying to enter. The case of sixteen-year-old Aboubakar Wada from Niger illustrates the tenacious resolve of many young Africans who arrive at the Spanish frontier. In November 2014 he crossed all three border fences at Melilla before being returned to Morocco by Spanish police. "I was thinking that I was finally in Spain," he said, "I'm not going back now to Niger, where there is nothing to do and no work, when every time I now wake up I can at least already see Europe."[53] Indeed, Niger is among the poorest countries in the world, with an average per capita annual income in 2014 of $427 (about $1.17 per day); by contrast, average per capita income in Morocco was $3,103, while in Spain it was nearly ten times higher at $30,262.[54] Spain, despite its high 26 percent unemployment rate and economic struggles since the Great Recession of 2008, seems rich in comparison.[55] The three countries illustrate well the essential difference between the core and periphery of the world-system.

Spanish police usually return Moroccans who attempt to enter Ceuta and Melilla illegally, but the situation is more complicated for migrants coming from farther afield. Sub-Saharan Africans often do not have travel documents, lose their papers along the way, give fake names, or lie about their nationality so as to make it hard for Spanish authorities to ascertain where they are from. The reason for this obfuscation is that Spain cannot send a person back if the country of origin is unknown or uncertain. If they try to discern whether a person is from Benin or Togo, getting any kind of response or verification from those countries is unlikely. As one exasperated official in Ceuta said, "you try calling Burundi. You try sending a fax to Sierra Leone. See how fast you get an answer."[56] According to European Union law, asylum seekers have the right to have their case heard by a court, which sometimes—depending on the particular circumstances—requires going to the mainland. When an application for political asylum is rejected, as most are, the person is not necessarily deported. Instead, they are given deportation papers and told to leave the country. Not surprisingly, they remain in Spain (or France, Italy, or Germany as the case may be) and live without proper residence permits in a sort of legal limbo.

Visions of Europe vary from person to person, but a common belief among Africans is that life is better there and everyone is comparatively wealthy. Cultural globalization has fostered a luxurious image of the Global North that is often detached from real day-to-day life. Migrants come with hopes of beginning a new life, earning money, and perhaps even getting rich. Often the plan is to send money back to relatives, many of whom have sacrificed to help the person get to Europe. The on-the-ground reality does not always match the original vision. The story of Babacar Diagne provides an example of someone who returned home without realizing the European dream. Having made it to Italy, he worked a variety of menial jobs in Corsica, Florence, and Genoa, but could still hardly pay his rent, let alone save enough to send any money back home. "At the time I really believed. Europe, the paradise," he said, only to conclude after spending twelve years there that "the Italians have changed. A few years ago, people helped out. But the whole atmosphere has become more hostile."[57] When he returned home to Senegal his relatives scolded him—where was the money for a house, a new fishing boat, tuition for his kids to go to school?—and people wondered why he had returned from Europe empty-handed.

In addition to the economic push and pull forces at work, Morocco plays a crucial political role in regulating how many migrants arrive in Spain. The Moroccan government can either help or hinder migrants on their way toward the Spanish outposts. In practice, it does both, depending on the state of international relations between the two countries. As one human rights activist put it, "Spain talks about having great cooperation with Morocco, but this cooperation is really just about paying Morocco to do the dirty work for Spain."[58] The "dirty work" comes in the form of harassing migrants who are leaving behind abject poverty, war zones, and failed states, who are in need of basic necessities like food, shelter, health care, and physical safety. Put simply, they are seeking a better life.

The discrepancy between the lives of Europeans living in Ceuta and Melilla and the lives of Africans on the other side of the barricade often seems surreal. This stark difference between haves and have-nots was captured by José Palazón in an iconic 2014 photo of two Spaniards in Melilla playing a leisurely round of golf on a lush green course lined with palm trees.[59] One player looks on as the other elegantly swings a golf club. In the background, a dozen Africans sit atop a six-meter wire fence separating Spain from Morocco. They are migrants waiting for the moment when they will simultaneously make the dangerous jump down off the fence and onto Spanish territory. It is a visual image that juxtaposes the opulence and luxury of the North against the desperation and poverty of the South. It symbolizes the economic gulf between Spain and Morocco, the wealth disparity between Europe and Africa, and the vast distance between core and periphery.

THE EUROPEAN UNION

In the bloody aftermath of World Wars I and II, which together killed close to 100 million people, Western European countries were ready to cooperate with each other in a spirit of enlightened self-interest. First steps toward political and economic cooperation in Western Europe included the creation of the Council of Europe in 1949 and the European Coal and Steel Community (ECSC) in 1952. The ECSC initially consisted of France, Germany, Italy, and the Benelux countries (Belgium, Netherlands, and Luxembourg), which became the nucleus of what is now the European Union. The goal was to inextricably bind the countries together so that they would have too much to lose economically if they went to war against each other, as France and Germany had done twice in the first half of the twentieth century. The plan worked, and the Community evolved rapidly. In March 1957 the original six countries signed the Treaty of Rome and established a common market known as the European Economic Community (EEC). The founding members stated that they were "determined to lay the foundations of an ever closer union among the peoples of Europe" and "resolved to ensure the economic and social progress of their countries by common action to eliminate the barriers which divide Europe."[60] This included the freedom of movement for goods, services, money, and (most important of all) people between the member states.

The European Economic Community grew from six members to nine as the United Kingdom, Ireland, and Denmark joined in 1973, followed by Greece in 1981, and Spain and Portugal in 1986. In this time of growth, enlargement, and increasing interdependence, the Single European Act further liberalized policies within not just a common market, but a single market "without internal frontiers in which the free movement of goods, persons, services and capital is ensured."[61] In addition to taking further steps toward a common currency, European citizenship was introduced in the 1992 Treaty of Maastricht, giving citizens of the Union "the right to move and reside freely within the territory of the Member States."[62] This spirit of cooperation occurred within the context of both the fall of the Berlin Wall and subsequent German unification, as well as the final dissolution of the Soviet Union and the subsequent expansion of the capitalist world-economy eastward.

France, Germany, and the Benelux countries met in the small town of Schengen, Luxembourg, to discuss abolishing internal border checks so that residents of the five countries could travel freely within the so-called Schengen Area. The town of Schengen was chosen deliberately, as it lies along the Mosel River on the border between France and Germany and symbolizes the coming together of the two major European countries. The Schengen Agreement went into effect in 1995 and, after being updated with the Treaty of Amsterdam in 1997, grew to include twenty-six countries. Some members of the European Union decided not to join Schengen out of choice (e.g., Ireland, the United Kingdom), and some could not join because they had not met the criteria for securing their external borders (Bulgaria, Cyprus, Romania), while others chose to be part of Schengen but not the European Union (Iceland, Norway, Switzerland). Nevertheless, the practical result today is a massive area stretching from Portugal to Poland and Iceland to Italy where travelers can cross international borders without having their passports checked. A flight from Austria to the Netherlands, for example, is today treated the same as a domestic flight.

Former EU Home Affairs commissioner Cecilia Malmström summed up the situation when she stated that Europeans take "over 1.25 billion journeys as tourists every year, and we can visit our friends and relatives all over Europe without bureaucratic obstacles at internal borders

. . . the creation of the Schengen Area is one of the most tangible, popular, and successful achievements of the EU."[63] Indeed, more than 400 million Europeans live in the Schengen zone and now have the freedom to move, settle, live, and work where they choose. Even non-EU citizens who are residing in Europe are able to travel unrestricted through the Schengen countries. It is undoubtedly among the most important progressive developments of the late twentieth and early twenty-first centuries regarding the processes of globalization and international migration.

This author can testify to the pleasant transformation the Schengen Agreement has brought to Europe. As an American studying in Groningen, the Netherlands, in 1988, I had to make a time-consuming and costly trip to the French embassy in Amsterdam in order to get a visa for a relatively short, week-long trip to France. The train ride from Amsterdam to Brussels and on to Paris truly felt, at the time, like an international journey from the windswept lowlands into the magnificent Francophone heart of Europe. Today the same trip is just as exhilarating, but the bureaucratic hassle of applying for a visa is nothing more than a nostalgic memory from a bygone era. The high-speed Thalys train now glides along the rails at 250 kilometers an hour and the conductor is, for the most part, interested only in whether passengers have valid tickets. Commuters act as if it is the most normal thing in the world to cruise unencumbered through three European countries within the span of only a few quick hours.

The great benefit of freedom of movement in the Schengen Area, however, brought with it at least two major challenges. The first, internal security, became increasingly significant after the September 11, 2001, terrorist attacks on the World Trade Towers and the Pentagon—two powerful symbols of American capitalism and war-making. In response, the United States and a coalition of European countries, including Britain, Holland, and Spain, started a ruinous war in Iraq that killed an estimated one million Iraqis and made refugees of millions more.[64] The cycle of violence continued on European soil with the March 2004 train bombings in Madrid and July 2007 underground bombings in London. Because most of the perpetrators in New York, Madrid, and London were Islamist extremists with immigrant backgrounds, these lethal attacks made international migration an unmistakable national security issue.

The second challenge, external border control, has proven to be more difficult than at first envisioned. From the beginning, the Schengen Agreement acknowledged the potential dangers: "In view of the risks in the fields of security and illegal immigration, the ministers and State secretaries underline the need for effective external border controls . . . the contracting parties must, in particular, promote the harmonization of working methods for border control and surveillance."[65] As events in recent years have demonstrated, effectively regulating the European Union's external borders—whether between Poland and the Ukraine, Greece and Turkey, Hungary and Serbia, or Spain and Morocco—has turned out to be a gargantuan task beyond the present capabilities of the individual member states and the Union as a whole.

The 2015 terrorist attacks in Paris brought these issues again to the fore of Europe's political agenda. In the wake of the violence, European leaders reacted with angry and at times pessimistic warnings about the future of the grand European project. President François Hollande said in a speech to a joint session of the French parliament that "if Europe doesn't control its external borders it is the return of national borders of walls and barbed wire . . . This would mean the dismantling of the European Union."[66] European Council president Donald Tusk echoed the sentiment by declaring that "without control on our external borders, Schengen will become history."[67] Dutch prime minister Mark Rutte continued the verbal barrage by invoking the continent's barbarian past and demanding that Greece's "completely porous" border with Turkey be sealed off immediately: "I want it shut. I don't care how this happens, whether it is through pressure from Europe or through other agreements, just as long as it happens. As we all know from the Roman Empire, big empires go down if the borders are not protected."[68] Prime Minister Rutte's proposed solution to the problem, rejected by nearly everyone, was to reduce the Schengen zone from twenty-six countries to a core of only five, consisting of the Netherlands, Belgium, Luxembourg, Germany, and Austria.

In addition to the Schengen Agreement coming under greater scrutiny, the 2015 arrival in Europe of more than a million asylum seekers all but shattered the Dublin III Regulation. According to Dublin III, an asylum seeker must apply for asylum in the first EU country that he or she enters. But this rule is often ignored. In reality, asylum seekers transit through Greece, Italy, or Spain (or Bulgaria, Romania, and Hungary,

as the case may be) on their way to the more affluent and orderly countries of northwestern Europe. According to the German magazine *Der
Spiegel*, perhaps only one of the 155 migrants who survived the October
3, 2013, shipwreck that killed 366 people within sight of Lampedusa,
stayed in Italy:

> Hardly anyone wants to stay in Italy, even though the country ap-
> proved 64 percent of asylum applications last year, more than twice
> the European Union average. Italy's refugee camps are overcrowded,
> forcing thousands of immigrants to live in the streets. Very few of these
> immigrants are working legally or receiving medical care, which is why
> they want to leave Italy for countries like Germany. That's a goal Italy
> is helping them achieve: More than a quarter of the refugees are not
> registered by the Italians, enabling them to apply for asylum wherever
> they choose—or wherever they are arrested.[69]

European countries have attempted to shift the responsibility of accept-
ing asylum seekers onto each other. This should not happen, according
to European Union law, but it does. Germany and Sweden appear to its
southern and eastern neighbors to be rich and generous, so the Italians,
Hungarians, and Greeks, for example, do not mind letting migrants
pass on to the north. Even the Austrians are content to let migrants
continue on to their larger Germanic neighbor. Migrants themselves
also prefer northern countries such as Germany, the Netherlands, and
Sweden because they have traditionally provided social services, adequate living conditions, and fair asylum hearings.

It should be noted that up to a million potential migrants are waiting on the shores of North Africa, and approximately four million
Syrian refugees are living in Turkey, Jordan, Lebanon, and elsewhere
in the Middle East. In theory, each refugee should be given adequate
shelter, health care, and food. But in practice, the member states of the
European Union have finite capacities and resources. Many are themselves economically stressed, and at a certain point compassion fatigue
sets in—the political will to take in foreigners diminishes among the
people. Bluntly stated, most Europeans do not want increased migration from outside the European Union, especially from countries to
the south and east commonly considered to fall outside the so-called
European "cultural sphere." Eurobarometer opinion polls from 2014
show that 57 percent of EU residents felt "immigration of people from

outside the EU" evoked a negative feeling.[70] In Greece, Italy, and Spain, this figure reached 75 percent. September 2015 polls showed that immigration had become the most prominent issue in Europe, ahead of the economic situation, unemployment, the state of public finances, terrorism, inflation, crime, and climate change.[71]

European Union member states have committed themselves to modern human rights norms, which are spelled out in official documents such as the Charter of Fundamental Rights. The European Union acknowledges, for instance, its spiritual and moral heritage and states in the Charter that it "is founded on the indivisible, universal values of human dignity, freedom, equality and solidarity; it is based on the principles of democracy and the rule of law. It places the individual at the heart of its activities, by establishing the citizenship of the Union and by creating an area of freedom, security and justice."[72] Nevertheless, mass migration poses great philosophical and practical challenges to the European Union, its individual member states, and its explicitly stated human rights principles. The question remains unsettled as to whether or not there will be an equitable sharing of the responsibility of taking in asylum seekers or a coordinated European Union solution to the refugee crisis at its external borders.

Let us now return to two final issues that have much to do with both the relationship between core and periphery, and the confluence of globalization and migration. The first, brain gain (the counterpart of brain drain), affects economic development in the Global North and continued underdevelopment in the Global South. The second, environmentally induced migration, is an emerging challenge that threatens to radically alter the course of world history in the twenty-first century.

BRAIN GAIN

In contrast to brain drain, brain gain occurs when a country attracts highly skilled migrants and thus acquires the all-important human capital necessary for developed economies to function. Educated people are in high demand in large part because knowledge and technology have become defining elements of our post-modern age. As Manuel Castells noted in *The Informational City* (1989), "a technological revolution of historic proportions is transforming the fundamental dimensions of human life: time and space. New scientific discoveries and industrial innovations are extending the productive capacity of working hours while superseding spatial distance in all realms of social activity."[73] Castells made this prescient observation at the very dawn of the Internet age, at a time when the process of globalization was accelerating.

For countries that receive skilled migrants, the benefits are abundant. Migrants with special skills fill gaps in the labor market and often do jobs that natives are unable or unqualified to do. Good examples of this are IT specialists, medical doctors, and scientists—in other words, as Jagdish Bhagwati puts it, "software engineers, not huddled masses."[74] The receiving country does not have to invest in the migrant's schooling or training, which was borne by the sending country. Rather, the migrant makes a contribution economically by being a taxpaying member of society and socially by adding to the overall human capital of the community. What is more, university-educated people are, on average, healthier, wealthier, happier, and more law-abiding than those who are not.[75]

Most significantly, brain gain gives economically developed countries an even greater advantage than they previously had and furthers the already wide gap between the rich and poor. Economist Stephen Moore has noted, for instance, that "in the twentieth century, between 20 percent and 50 percent of the Nobel Prize winners, depending on the discipline involved, have been immigrants to the United States . . . There are more Russian Nobel Prize winners living in the U.S. than there are living in Russia."[76] An extensive 2012 study examined four decades of literature on brain drain migration and concluded "globalization is making human capital scarcer where it is already scarce and more abundant where it is already abundant, thereby contributing to increasing inequality across countries, including among the richer ones."[77] Moreover, the study indicated that brain drain is not happening by accident. It is the result of intentional policies crafted by national governments in a global race to attract the best and brightest people. Whether it is European states attracting medical professionals from Africa, the United States hiring European scientists, or Canadians recruiting Indian computer specialists, it is clear that there is a global competition for talent and that the core countries of the Global North are winning.

However, educated migrants are beneficial to the receiving country in most but not all cases. It sometimes happens that skilled migrants are unable to put their knowledge to good use. Language proficiency barriers may stop them from communicating well enough to get and keep a job. Authenticating, translating, and recognizing a person's qualifications may be difficult as well, and lead to the unfortunate scenario of a former teacher being forced to make ends meet by driving a taxi. In this instance, so-called "brain waste" refers not to spending five hours in front of the television every night, but to the inability of highly qualified immigrants to put their skills to use in their host countries.[78]

CLIMATE CHANGE

According to Camilo Mora, a biogeographer studying the effects of global warming, the year 2047 will be the "year of climate change departure" in which global temperatures will rise to searing levels and extreme heat will be the norm. "If you do not like it hot and do not want to be hit by a hurricane, the options of where to go are very limited," he says, "the best place really is Alaska."[79] Professor Mora belongs to an overwhelming majority of climate scientists who agree the planet is in for major changes in the twenty-first century. The hottest places in the United States are expected to be in southern states like California, Arizona, New Mexico, and Texas, while the coolest and most livable areas are predicted to be in the Pacific Northwest and Alaska. "The Pacific Ocean is like our natural air conditioning," says Clifford Mass, an atmospheric science professor at the University of Washington, adding that "water is important, and we will have it."[80] These favorable conditions are likely to attract millions of future climate change migrants from within the United States as well as Mexico, Central America, and elsewhere in the Global South.

A 2009 report by the UNHCR and Columbia University's Earth Institute on the link between climate change and migration suggests that people in less developed regions are most likely to be hit "first and worst," and "may find themselves locked into a downward spiral of ecological degradation, toward the bottom of which social safety nets collapse while tensions and violence rise. In this all-too-plausible worst-case scenario, large populations would be forced to migrate as a matter of immediate survival."[81] Migrants moving north from adversely affected regions in Central America would, for example, have to cross the 1,954-mile border separating Mexico and the United States and potentially be considered "climate refugees." So, too, would Africans and

Middle Easterners crossing the Mediterranean en route to Europe, and Pacific Islanders from Oceania migrating to Australia and New Zealand.

The term "refugee" is laden with historical and political meaning. In the aftermath of World War II, which displaced tens of millions of people, the United Nations set about codifying the concept in the 1951 Geneva Convention Relating to the Status of Refugees. Article 1 of the Convention defines a refugee as any person who "owing to a well-founded fear of being persecuted for reasons of race, religion, nationality, membership of a particular social group or political opinion, is outside the country of his nationality and is unable or, owing to such a fear, is unwilling to avail himself of the protection of that country."[82] The original definition was limited to events in Europe occurring before 1951, but these geographic and temporal restrictions were lifted in an amendment known as the 1967 Protocol. As of 2015, 142 countries had signed both the 1951 Convention and its 1967 Protocol.

Hence, the internationally accepted United Nations definition makes no mention of environmental disasters or climate change as grounds for refugee status. Amending it to account for climate refugees will presumably be problematic. For one, it is difficult to determine who qualifies, because the reasons for forced migration are usually multiple, intertwined, and complex. In many cases it is hard to say definitively what caused a person to migrate: was it the war that was brought on by the struggle over natural resources, which was due to famine-related crop failure, which was caused by the lack of water resulting from the decade-long drought, which was a result of climate change? States that already receive large numbers of migrants, including asylum seekers and refugees, are wary of broadening the UN refugee definition, as it would lead to yet more immigration. Moreover, the number of future climate refugees is potentially enormous. Estimates range from the tens to hundreds of millions, but these are admittedly educated guesses based on speculation about what the future will bring—such as Professor Mora's model predicting 2047 will be the tipping point.

CONCLUSION

To return to the initial question at the beginning of the chapter, why do so many people migrate to the Global North? In comparative perspective, rich core countries offer jobs, educational opportunity, social mobility, stable government, and political freedoms. The European Union is viewed with good reason as a thriving, prosperous, and peaceful haven. The obvious attraction of the United States and Canada is apparent in their large national economies, democratic institutions, and ability to absorb immigrants into society. Similarly, the dream of moving to Australia and New Zealand is so powerful that, in some cases, migrants are willing to risk their lives to get there. But, as we have seen in the preceding chapters, there are larger historical and structural forces at work. Five hundred years of expansion of the capitalist market, of colonialism, of core development and periphery underdevelopment, have shaped the world in which we currently live.

Globalization has dislocated millions of people and set in motion population movements that are now hard for anyone or anything to control. This represents a serious political challenge to nation-states, which remain among the most powerful actors in world politics. When they can no longer effectively regulate who crosses their borders, either because they are practically unable to enforce immigration laws or lack the resolve to do so, it raises the critical question of whether national boundaries are on the way to obsolescence. To the extent that this is, indeed, occurring, a rethinking of the concept of the nation-state with its population, territory, and institutions, as well as complex issues relating to national identity and citizenship, will be necessary.

When these pillars of traditional political thought are reconsidered, we may then arrive at a point where, as Marx and Engels wrote long ago, "all fixed, fast-frozen relations, with their train of ancient and venerable prejudices and opinions, are swept away, all new-formed ones become antiquated before they can ossify. All that is solid melts into air, all that is holy is profaned, and man is at last compelled to face with sober senses, his real conditions of life, and his relations with his kind."[83] For at its core global migration is not just about politics and economics, it is about human rights and ethics. It raises fundamental questions for the international community: Should people be able to cross international borders, especially when they are fleeing conflict, escaping the worst effects of climate change, living in abject poverty, in need of work, hoping to join a relative who has emigrated, or merely because they see more promising opportunities abroad? More broadly, how shall we live together on this planet, and how shall we organize ourselves so that we can achieve the greatest good for the greatest number of people?

CHAPTER 5

THE COMING TRANSFORMATION

"The majority of Tuvaluans have this concept that Tuvalu will eventually go under water," said Afa'ese Manoa, founder of New Zealand's Pacific Island Climate Change Action Forum. "Everyone's trying to facilitate the process of moving."[1] Situated halfway between Australia and Hawaii, Tuvalu has 11,000 inhabitants living on nine low-lying coral atolls and may indeed be the first country in the world to disappear. Rising ocean water is already apparent and doing damage, especially when the "king tides" roll in or major storms pass through. Gardens are being rendered unusable by encroaching saltwater that ruins arable soil and prevents vegetables from growing. Waves are splashing up against public buildings and eroding their foundations. Roads are being flooded over. The people are adapting by moving to higher ground and building berms, but they are also migrating to Fiji and nearby island countries. After Cyclone Pam slammed Tuvalu in March 2015, half the island's residents were displaced. One in five Tuvaluans now lives abroad, mostly in New Zealand, where the community struggles to come to terms with its dislocation.

Sigeo Alesana left Tuvalu in 2007 with his wife and mother and moved to New Zealand, where his five sisters had also immigrated. When his visitor visa ran out he applied for work and residence visas, which were denied. Although Mr. Alesana is a qualified teacher, he was unable to regularize his immigration status and thus fell into the "unlawful resident" category. As a last resort, he and his wife and two young New Zealand–born children applied for refugee status, claiming they could not return to Tuvalu due to the harmful effects of climate change. Their case was dismissed and their first appeal turned down, but they appealed a second time and in June 2014 were allowed to stay on humanitarian grounds. New Zealand's Immigration and Protection Tribunal reasoned that because of "exceptional circumstances" it would be "unjust and unduly harsh" to send the family back.[2] The tribunal accepted the following argument: "The appellants claim that if deported to Tuvalu they will be separated from the husband's family, all of whom are living in New Zealand as either citizens or residents, and with whom they have particularly close bonds. The appellants also claim that they will be at risk of suffering the adverse impacts of climate change and socioeconomic deprivation."[3] The decision was noteworthy because it so distinctly acknowledged the consequences of environmental damage on Tuvalu. It recognized that life on the islands has become more difficult, that they are overcrowded and "increasingly more vulnerable to inundation by seawater as a result of sea-level rise."[4] Following the ruling, the first of its kind in the world, international observers wondered whether the era of the "climate change refugee" had begun.[5]

Tuvalu is not alone. People living in island nations such as Kiribati, Palau, and the Maldives, to name but a few, are also dealing with rising sea levels that are harming water supplies, arable land, and crops. According to Peter Sinclair, a geoscientist working in the South Pacific, the consequences could be dire. "If current trajectories persist," he says, "millions of Pacific islanders will continue to endure unsafe water and sanitation for generations to come, with profound implications for economic growth, public health, the environment and human rights."[6] This forecast applies generally to more than just Pacific islanders, who in global comparative perspective are relatively few in number. Many more people face similar climate-related dangers in places such as the Sahel region in Africa, the Philippines, the Ganges Delta in Bangladesh, and the Mekong Delta in Vietnam. Residents of European and American cities such as Venice, Amsterdam, London, New York, New Orleans, and Miami are also seeing rising tides and increasingly fierce storms. Yet the difference is that in Tuvalu, Kiribati, Palau, and elsewhere in the South Pacific, some islands are already disappearing. Unlike the technologically savvy Dutch or the rich Americans, the Tuvaluans have few options. They can try to adapt, or leave, or convince the international community's largest polluters to stop spewing harmful greenhouse gases into the atmosphere. They can make their case using the soft power of persuasion, as Tuvaluan prime minister Enele Sopoaga did at the December 2014 United Nations Climate Summit when he asked: "If you were faced with the threat of the disappearance of your nation, what would you do?"[7]

THE GATHERING STORM

This concluding chapter looks ahead at possible future scenarios and provides an opportunity to contemplate a number of larger questions about globalization and migration. Can economic globalization be reined in before it uproots and dislodges even more people than it already has? Is it possible to effectively control large-scale migration in an age of intensifying global interdependence, interconnectedness, ethnic conflict, and climate change? Are open borders a realistic scenario? And where is our Global Village heading? Before getting to these questions, however, let me first offer some reflections in light of what has been said in the preceding chapters.

In the year in which this book was written a variety of issues related to globalization and migration made front-page news on a near daily basis. In 2015 the headlines seemed to announce one tragedy after the next, such as the tens of thousands of unaccompanied children arriving at America's southern border; Burmese and Bangladeshi refugees stranded at sea; and thousands of migrant deaths in the Mediterranean. Paris was twice attacked by terrorists with immigrant backgrounds, killing twelve people in January and 130 people in November, and all the while the exodus of Afghans, Iraqis, and Syrians out of the war-ravaged Middle East and into the European Union continued. Scientists declared it was the hottest year ever recorded, far surpassing the previous year's record-setting levels. Even Pope Francis weighed in by eloquently calling for every parish in Europe to take in at least one refugee family and issuing an encyclical on climate change that urged us to "hear the cry of the earth and the cry of the poor."[8] The stories unfolded at such a rapid pace it reminded me of an edition of the Russian newspaper *Pravda* at the height of the Bolshevik Revolution that one day simply said, "No news today. Events happening too fast."[9] Indeed, the unrelenting refugee crisis at times made me put down my pen with a sigh and wonder about the uncertain future of our globalized world.

Much of this writing was done at the University of Vienna in Austria, where I lived in the 10th District immigrant neighborhood of Favoriten. The 10th District itself is a rich case study in migration, for in the late nineteenth century it attracted thousands of Bohemian manual laborers who came to work (up to fifteen hours a day, seven days a week, for low pay) in the brick factories in that southern suburb of the metropolis. Nowadays when you walk through the streets of Favoriten and through the Viktor-Adler Markt you may not always hear German being spoken, but rather a mix of Arabic, Croatian, Hungarian, Serbian, Turkish, and other languages. The striking thing about the neighborhood is that it has a long history of attracting immigrants who have at first mixed uneasily with each other but ultimately left their cultural mark on the place. Today a pastime of the descendants of the earlier Bohemian migrants is to gather in local bars and cafés and complain—without the slightest hint of irony—about the influx of foreigners who seem so strange with their burkas and headscarves and foreign manners. It makes one wonder what people a hundred years hence will be talking about and who the newcomers then will be.

When I look at my own life, having moved frequently around the United States and having lived a handful of years in Europe and Africa, I see clearly that migration is virtually everywhere a visible social reality. There have been migrants in every country and city I have ever visited and, of course, I myself have been a migrant. Yet, as one would expect, the dynamics of globalization and migration have changed over the years. When I was growing up my family spent a good deal of time in the summer months picking cherries and apples in the state of Washington. In the 1970s and early 1980s it seemed to me the workers were mostly poor whites—hippies who picked fruit in the summer and tried to live off the grid for the rest of the year. They were simple folks who sat around the campfire at night telling fantastic stories of American life, who had said no to the Vietnam War, and who got only the meager leftovers of Ronald Reagan's "trickle down" economics. Hispanics who worked in the orchards then were a minority, and the contact between them and the Anglo workers was minimal due primarily to the mutual inability to speak the other's language. Neither group was part of a workers' union. Today most of the white fruit pickers are gone and a predominately Mexican migrant workforce does the bulk of the picking, pruning, and harvesting. Most of the landowners are still Anglo-American, but the number of small family-owned orchards has dwindled. They have been replaced by larger, much more corporate operations that grow fruit on an industrial scale and require imported labor to harvest it.

This personal anecdote is one small example of how migrant workers are needed to do physically demanding and poorly paid jobs that natives in the Global North are either unable or unwilling to do. Working in the heat all day for minimum wage and no benefits is hard, and few Americans today will do it. Still, the fruits and vegetables need to be picked. We all have to eat, and the way in which food ends up on our plates says a lot about us and our societal values. Were the workers who harvested the food treated fairly and paid a living wage? Was the food sprayed with harmful chemicals as it grew? How far was it shipped before it was sold to consumers? The answers to these questions reveal a set of discomfiting issues. In most cases, no, migrant farmworkers are not treated fairly. They tend to live in poverty on the margins of society and are exploited by agricultural corporations motivated by the endless pursuit of profit. Their efforts to unionize—an act that would give them more bargaining power and rights—are often hindered and thwarted. The food they pick is produced on such a massive scale and sold so cheaply that small family farms cannot compete. Mom-and-pop operations then go under, or are bought out and their land consolidated into bigger farms. The fertilizers and toxic pesticides that are heaped onto the soil and plants not only kill bugs, but also seep into the ground and generally do damage to the ecosystem. Food is regularly shipped across continents and oceans and consumed half a world away by people who do not know or care where it came from or how much fossil fuel was burned in order to transport it to them.

Then there is the issue of race. Nonwhite migrant laborers are rarely welcomed in countries that have majority white populations. In Australia, Europe, and North America—to name but a few places—ethnic tension and outright racism lurk in the shadows of society and occasionally rear their ugly heads. In the United States, hateful speech could be heard on the campaign trail in the summer of 2015 when Republican billionaire Donald Trump announced his candidacy for president of the United States with a slanderous tirade against immigrants. "When Mexico sends its people, they're not sending their best. They're not sending you," he told an enthusiastic crowd of supporters, "they're sending people that have lots of problems . . . they're bringing drugs, they're bringing crime. They're rapists... It's coming from more than Mexico. It's coming from all over South and Latin America, and it's coming probably—probably—from the Middle East."[10] Trump rambled on incoherently and then unveiled his immigration policy plan: "I would build a great wall, and nobody builds walls better than me, believe me, and I'll build them very inexpensively, I will build a great, great wall on our southern border. And I will have Mexico pay for that wall."[11] This despicable, half-witted rhetoric catapulted Donald Trump into the lead among likely Republican voters. American nativists apparently liked what they heard.

The remaining field of Republican presidential candidates mostly tried to outdo one another as to who, if elected, would be toughest on border control, who would deport more undocumented migrants, and who would be first to change the Fourteenth Amendment to the Constitution (which guarantees citizenship to children born on U.S. soil). Union-busting Wisconsin governor Scott Walker even entertained the ridiculous idea of building a wall along the 5,525-mile border between the United States and Canada.[12] What no candidate dared to say is that there has never been a golden age of immigration control when foreigners were effectively shut out of the United States. Such tight regulation has never been realistic considering how vast America's sea and land borders are. Ingenious and determined migrants will always find ways over, under, or around fences and walls. Even if it were possible to stop international migration, businesses would not stand for it because the capitalist world-system relies so heavily on cheap labor. Powerful, politically connected lobbyists would demand the pool of reserve workers be made available, and corporate governments would comply. Here we arrive at a truism of immigration: nativist arguments about the need to preserve national identity nearly always lose out in the end to the more powerful capitalist demand for labor.

Despite protestations by those who would prefer to conserve traditional culture in Europe and North America, legal and illegal migration continues unabated. It often leads citizens of countries that receive large numbers of immigrants to ask foreigners in their midst, "Who are you, why are you here, where did you come from, and how did you get here?" It compels people to examine themselves and their country, to think about their personal and national identities and to ask existential questions like, "Who Are We?"[13] At an individual level, it pushes people to examine their relationship to those around them, especially to newcomers who seem strange, different, and "other." At the societal level it begs the question, "How shall we then live together?" At the state level, policymakers must deal with questions of what is in the best interest of the country in economic, social, and political terms. At the global level, intergovernmental organizations are confronted with labor migration and the crushing problem of refugees and displaced persons.

The United Nations does excellent work on behalf of migrants and those who are weak, vulnerable, and do not have a voice. In the face of serious global problems, however, it uses the well-mannered language of diplomacy. The UNHCR, for example, calls on "European governments to address the problem of people fleeing wars" and encourages "more focus on addressing the root causes of population movements."[14] It gently recommends that the global community solve its messy problems, and it is undoubtedly right to do so, but often these appeals fall on deaf ears. The harsh reality is such that there is so much war, poverty, and oppression that millions of people would, if they could, migrate from the poor to rich regions of the world. According to a 2014 poll, for instance, more than one-third of all Mexicans would move to the United States if they had the means and opportunity to do so.[15] Yet there are, ultimately, practical limits with regard to space, finite budgets, infrastructure, and tolerance of foreigners in receiving countries. At this point in history, state sovereignty is a reality that makes open borders an idea whose time has not yet come.

The international system that has emerged as of the early twenty-first century is tilted strongly in favor of the nation-states and citizens of the Global North. People who have the financial means may travel, invest in property abroad, and even buy citizenship. Those who are willing and able to invest 1.15 million euros in Malta (a member of the European Union since 2004), for example, can get citizenship there, and similar schemes for the super-rich exist in the United Kingdom, Canada, and the United States. Talented, well-educated, and rich people tend to be highly mobile in the current age of globalization. Wealthy investors are welcomed everywhere. Yet such people represent only a tiny fraction of the world's seven billion people. The majority of the global population is comparatively poor and does not have the money to travel exclusively by plane or the wherewithal to navigate through the confusing forest of paperwork necessary to migrate legally. Thus, the cumulative advantages of the rich continue to increase the gap between the Global North and South.

As the wealthy countries of the world try to insulate themselves from the poverty, war, and dysfunction all around them, powerful storms are gathering on the horizon. Environmental destruction could cause hundreds of millions of people to move out of the hardest hit places, likely in the Global South. The outlines of such a scenario are already visible in the form of rising ocean levels, flooding, melting glaciers, shrinking polar ice caps, deforestation, desertification, severe drought, ocean acidification, air pollution, super storms, and record-setting rises in average global temperatures. The crucial question is whether enough nation-states will react to the looming global environmental catastrophe in time to stave off the climate refugee crisis that is sure to follow. Unfortunately, current policies in Europe and North America suggest that we are likely to see a mix of procrastination on climate policy, stricter immigration laws, militarization of border areas, and more war over dwindling natural resources. If this indeed turns out to be the case, planet earth and all its inhabitants face a future in which potentially huge numbers of people will be forced to migrate.

WHAT IS TO BE DONE?

As citizens of the world we must all recognize the damage neoliberal economic policies are doing to human beings and the planet. Residents of the Global North have a special responsibility in this regard, for their countries have contributed disproportionately to the harm that is being done. At the same time they are in a strong position to make their democratically elected governments pursue peaceful, environmentally sustainable, economically just policies. An important step toward making the world a more livable place, however, involves getting our collective priorities straight. What is more important, feeding the hungry or repaying investors? Taking in refugees or building more bombs? Cutting carbon emissions or drilling for more oil? The answers to these and similar questions are crucial. If we choose militarism and greed, the result will likely be more poverty, armed conflict, extreme weather events, and mass forced migration. If, on the other hand, we choose humanitarianism and sustainability, we may just transition to a more humane phase of life on the planet.

What will such an age of positive transition entail and how can it be achieved? First, economic globalization must be brought under democratic control. The current global economy is geared to work in favor of corporations, stockholders, and the wealthy instead of the poor. Multinational corporations have become so rich and powerful that they dictate to politicians what policy should be. Predictably, they lobby hard for lower taxes and fewer regulations—and that is precisely what they get from compliant policymakers who are later handsomely repaid for doling out political favors. It should, of course, be the other way around. The people should dictate policies to governments and corporations, and democratically elected policymakers should close loopholes and offshore tax havens that allow big business to pay little or nothing back to society. According to the human rights organization Oxfam International, in 2010 some 388 billionaires owned as much wealth as 3.5 billion of the poorest people on earth, and by 2015 a mere 80 individuals owned as much as half of all humanity.[16] Put another way, 1 percent of the global population has as much wealth as the other 99 percent. Much of the corruption, graft, and fraud that enabled this extreme concentration of wealth occurred in the three decades between 1985 and 2015 when the super-rich got even richer and economic inequality reached levels unprecedented in human history. To my mind this development is ethically unconscionable and it is time for the 99 percent to take nonviolent revolutionary action. In the interest of global social justice, the citizens of the world need to use democratic means and progressive tax laws to radically redistribute the hoarded wealth of the billionaires back to the poor, the malnourished, the sick, and the asylum seekers.

Second, global military spending is harmful to our collective health and well-being. Money that is misspent on weapons represents a grave threat to humankind. American president Dwight Eisenhower said it well back in 1953: "Every gun that is made, every warship launched, every rocket fired signifies, in the final sense, a theft from those who hunger and are not fed, those who are cold and are not clothed. The world in arms is not spending money alone. It is spending the sweat of its laborers, the genius of its scientists, the hopes of its children."[17] Tragically, Eisenhower was all but ignored in the half-century after he made this extraordinary statement. Despite his warning about the unwarranted influence and danger of the growing military industrial complex, the international arms race spiraled out of control. Multinational corporations made vast fortunes manufacturing all manner of deadly weapons that have fueled countless wars around the world. The result has been near continual warfare and millions dead, wounded, and dislocated.

It is time to bring the weapons industry under strict regulatory control. This may sound quixotic, but it is possible and urgently necessary. Democratically passed laws could quickly stop the manufacture and sale of weapons in the United States, Germany, France, the United Kingdom, Spain, and Italy—which together produced more than half of all weapons sold worldwide from 2010 to 2014.[18] What is required is the political will to stand up to multinational corporations that make weapons, profit from war, and deal in death. These include Boeing, Lockheed Martin, Raytheon, BAE Systems, and Northrop Grumman. Voters in the Global North, where most of the weapons are made, must realize that the military industrial complex is detrimental to their societies and to others. It not only kills people, it wastes money that could otherwise be spent on productive activities like providing health care and education, building schools and hospitals, supporting the arts and sciences. War may be profitable for an elite few in the upper echelons of the military, but it is catastrophic for everyone else. Most importantly, there is no sane use for nuclear weapons, for they are designed to annihilate life on earth.

Third, climate justice must be made a top priority. A massive, already long overdue global green revolution is needed. This would include transitioning from burning fossil fuels to using renewable wind, solar, and hydroelectric energy; a colossal push toward environmental sustainability; an immediate stop to practices that destroy forests, oceans, and wildlife habitat. Failure to use renewables, to live sustainably, to live in harmony with the earth will almost certainly transform civilization for the worse. People will be forced to move due to the life-changing effects of climate change. Farmers will migrate if they cannot eke out a living when their water sources dry up and irretrievably disappear or when forests are clear-cut and the soil erodes. Coastal dwellers will abandon their homes when rising water levels flood villages and powerful hurricanes wipe out whole cities.

Fourth, the United Nations needs the full support of all countries, but especially its most wealthy and powerful members. Despite the UN's imperfections, its aim is to improve the human condition and prevent war. The vast majority of its programs, funds, offices, and specialized agencies do an immeasurable amount of good. The World Health Organization, World Food Programme, Children's Fund, Environment Programme, Women's Fund, and High Commission for Refugees are but a small sampling of the institutions working to help the world's most vulnerable people. They provide feasible ways to address the root causes of many of our most pressing social, economic, political, and environmental problems.

In September 2015 the United Nations Development Programme (UNDP) introduced a set of seventeen Sustainable Development Goals, which are an extension of the eight Millennium Development Goals of fifteen years earlier. At the unveiling of the new Global Goals the UNDP explained the predicament of our globalized world at the turn of the century and offered a vision of what is possible:

> In 2000, 189 countries of the world came together to face the future. And what they saw was daunting. Famines. Drought. Wars. Plagues. Poverty. The perennial problems of the world. Not just in some faraway place, but in their own cities and towns and villages. They knew things didn't have to be this way. They knew we had enough food to feed the world, but that it wasn't getting shared. They knew there were medicines for HIV and other diseases, but that they cost a lot. They knew that earthquakes and floods were inevitable, but that the high death tolls were not. They also knew that billions of people worldwide shared their hope for a better future . . . Now these countries want to build on the many successes of the past 15 years, and go further. The new set of goals, the Sustainable Development Goals (SDGs) aims to end poverty and hunger by 2030. World leaders, recognizing the connection between people and planet,

have set goals for the land, the oceans and the waterways. The world is also better connected now than it was in 2000, and is building a consensus about the future we want. That future is one where everybody has enough food, and can work, and where living on less than $1.25 a day is a thing of the past.[19]

The Sustainable Development Goals address issues ranging from poverty, hunger, health, and education to gender equality, clean water, and energy. A new emphasis has been placed on responsible consumption and production, climate action, sustainability, inequality, and peace. There are arguably few better ways to provide the greatest amount of good for the greatest number of people than to support the United Nations Global Goals.

Fifth, we must radically reallocate money from the military and the super-rich to social welfare and educational programs that promote peace and democratic values. To transform the capitalist world-system and make our global economy more just—for people, living things, and the planet itself—we will have to change our value system. Peace, for example, is not merely the absence of war, as the soldier and the state have traditionally told us. It is much more than that. In its full sense, positive peace means having food, shelter, and health care, as well as a healthy environment for children to grow up in, opportunities for self-fulfillment, artistic expression, well-being, and happiness. It means having loving human relationships, thriving communities, and respect for nature and Mother Earth. Cultivation of the intellect is the key to creating societal values that will provide a sustainable economy, a democracy that serves the 99 percent, and a world free of war.

Yet what is the likelihood that such changes will occur on a global scale? Perhaps more importantly, what will the consequences be if we fail to get our priorities straight? Will the world continue on its current path, constrained by decisions made in earlier decades and unable to shake free of the momentum driving the planet toward environmental collapse? Will a worst-case scenario emerge in which global environmental, economic, and political ruin occurs more precipitously than imagined? Or will a very great vision of globalization be realized in which we take the necessary steps to control runaway capitalism and militarism, and start caring for the planet, the children, and the least among us? In sum, what will the coming transformation look like?

CONCLUSION

It is often easiest to maintain the status quo rather than make serious changes. So it may turn out to be with the dual processes of globalization and migration. In this path-dependent scenario, the countries of the world stay locked on the present course as if stuck in a rut. The courageous leaders of countries that call for real change are stymied by the entrenched power of global elites, multinational corporations, and the military industrial complex. The wealthy countries do very little to alter the current dynamics of economic globalization, so that the rich continue to get richer and the poor poorer. Climate change continues and people in the Global North do not change their unsustainable ways of living—much like the proverbial frog that stays put because it does not notice the water is warming and will soon come to a boil. Rather, they build bigger fences and take ever-greater security measures to keep out masses of migrants who have left their impoverished, drought-stricken, war-torn homes.

Migrants who penetrate wealthy countries' borders face marginalization and deportation. Those who stay illegally live on the fringes of society and get caught in cycles of crime, poverty, and downward assimilation. The wealthy can afford to pay for their nannies, gardeners, and minimum-wage help, yet abject poverty remains for billions of people worldwide. The brutality of the global economic system, which relies on a vast reserve of cheap labor, continues. The richest billionaires—the Gates, Buffetts, Slims, Kochs, and Waltons, to name but a handful—continue amassing ever more wealth while the poorest half of humanity struggles to feed itself living hand-to-mouth on less than two dollars a day. Denial about the causes and imminent danger of global climate change continues as prominent politicians downplay the risks and the largest polluters pay nothing more than lip service to the idea that carbon emissions need to be curbed. Political gridlock leads to inaction followed by a classic case of the tragedy of the global commons.

A second possible scenario is much darker, yet very real. Population growth accelerates and surpasses ten billion before mid-century. The planet is grossly overcrowded, reaches its carrying capacity, and a humanitarian disaster unfolds. Everything worsens far quicker than imagined. Diseases, viruses, and superbugs spread in unforeseen ways that sicken and kill large numbers of people in the prime of their lives, which weakens the fabric of societies around the world. Volatile economic markets crash, once and for all, and wipe out the life savings of the middle class everywhere. As usual, the poor are hit hardest and bear the brunt of the economic meltdown. Storms become increasingly powerful and droughts more intense. A series of negative feedback loops emerge, leading to an out-of-control downward spiral: rising temperatures cause more forest fires, which produce more smoke in the atmosphere, which intensifies the global greenhouse effect, which melts glaciers faster, which causes sea levels to rise, which dislocates even more people.

One state fails after another. Conflict increases and wars break out. Nuclear weapons go unaccounted for and it is only a matter of time before one is detonated. The fallout resembles Rachel Carson's *Silent Spring*, when the birds disappear and are no longer heard chirping in the springtime. An exodus of hundreds of millions of people out of the Global South leads to a fortress mentality in the Global North, where countries implement draconian border control measures and devote ever more resources to mass deportations of foreigners. Those with the means to do so fortify themselves in a world where the police state uses drones and robots to impose a bizarre semblance of order. Big Brother arrives a half-century later than George Orwell predicted as armies and navies are used to violently repel masses of people trying to cross from Africa into Europe, Central into North America, and Asia into Australia. Advanced technology such as eye scans and biometric data are used to identify and track people. Children look up at their bewildered parents and ask, "How did this happen?"

A third potential scenario is one in which people around the world recognize that war, sickness, hunger, and forced migration are all unnecessary. Faced with the threat of global economic, political, and environmental collapse, they start to look deeply at their collective problems and contemplate what kind of a global society they really want to live in. They imagine a world that is healthy for all living beings and begin to work earnestly toward their goals. Globalization leads to greater international cooperation and an age of reason emerges characterized by a renaissance in scientific thinking. At long last, the root causes of forced migration are addressed as economic exploitation and poverty are mitigated. The burning of fossil fuels is dramatically reduced and the world's energy needs are met by switching to renewable solar, wind, and geothermal sources. Fighting over oil comes to an end along with the iniquitous phenomenon of petro-authoritarianism, where countries overly reliant on oil for their national income regress toward authoritarian government. The international arms trade is brought to an immediate halt, so that weapons are neither bought nor sold on the global market. Military budgets are slashed—at first by half and then by 90 percent—as the military industrial complex is brought to heel. Wars become a terrible memory of an earlier age of barbarism and the vast amount of money once wasted on them is directed to human welfare projects, modern infrastructure, and peace education.

The global population plateaus, then declines, and ultimately reaches a sustainable long-term equilibrium. Children brought into the world are eagerly welcomed by whole communities and given all the support necessary to lead long and fulfilling lives. There is enough food in the world to feed everyone and it is distributed so that as little as possible goes to waste. As a result, malnourishment becomes rare. Those who desire to migrate from one country to another can do so as free movement becomes accepted internationally. The subsequent mixing of peoples and human diversity minimizes ethnic tension over time. Global consciousness manifests itself in new international norms, or accepted standards of behavior, so that it becomes unthinkable that governments would misspend money on war when they could invest in health care and environmental protection. Just as the international community no longer accepts slavery, denying the vote to women, or institutionalized racism (as it once did in the nineteenth and twentieth centuries), it no longer accepts harmful neoliberal economic policies, war as a means of solving international disputes, or restricted freedom of movement.

A new generation emerges that has grown up in a borderless world and is acutely aware of the dangerous effects of unequal wealth distribution. Whereas earlier generations once shrugged their shoulders and accepted that eighty individual billionaires owned as much wealth as 3.5 billion people, the young find such extreme inequality completely unacceptable. Through democratic means they put an end to secret bank accounts, eliminate offshore tax havens, and use progressive policies to redistribute wealth from the rich to the poor. They intuitively understand the logic of strong workers' unions and swiftly put an end to exploitive labor conditions. Instead of paying their best and brightest to build nuclear weapons, the younger generation invests in scientific research and an international program dedicated to deep space exploration. The time inevitably comes when they migrate off planet and go boldly, like their ancient seafaring ancestors who set out in search of new worlds, into the immense darkness of space with an insatiable curiosity and an unshakeable belief that we are not alone in the universe.

NOTES

CHAPTER 1

1. Ali Najaf is a pseudonym. Krasimir Yankov won a journalism award for this insightful reportage, which appeared in German as "2000 Euro für den Schlepper," *Der Standard*, 17–18 January 2015. See also Krasimir Yankov, "Syrian Refugees Leave Bulgaria for German Limbo," *Erste Stiftung*, http://www.erstestiftung.org/blog/syrian-refugees-leave-bulgaria-for-german-limbo/ (accessed 24 January 2015).

2. Pegida is short for Patriotische Europäer gegen die Islamisierung des Abendlandes.

3. Bundesamt für Migration und Flüchtlinge, "Bis zu 800,000 Asylbewerber Erwartet," 19 August 2015, http://www.bamf.de/SharedDocs/Meldungen/DE/2015/20150819-BM-zur-Asylprognose.html (accessed 28 October 2015).

4. "Pegida-Demo nachTerror in Frankreich: 'Schlimm, das in Paris, aber . . .'" *Der Spiegel Online,* 13 January 2015, http://www.spiegel.de/politik/deutschland/

pegida-die-erste-demo-in-dresden-nach-dem-terror-in-paris-a-1012653.html (accessed 25 January 2015).

5. Heather Saul, "Nigel Farage Urges the West to Admit Some 'Culpability' in the Charlie Hebdo Attacks," *The Independent*, 13 January 2015.

6. Marine Le Pen, "To Call This Threat by Its Name," *International New York Times*, 19 January 2015.

7. Henry Chu, "'Please, Please! Stop!' Concertgoers Pleaded as Paris Theater Came Under Siege," *Los Angeles Times*, 14 November 2015, http://www.latimes.com/world/la-fg-paris-attacks-theater-20151114-story.html (accessed 14 November 2015).

8. Paul Armstrong and Brian Walker, "French President Blames ISIS for Terror Attacks," *CNN News*, 14 November 2015, http://www.cnn.com/2015/11/13/europe/paris-attacks-francois-hollande/ (accessed 14 November 2015).

9. "Confirming Death, France Laments Lack of Intelligence Sharing Over Paris Suspect's Movements," *PBS Newshour*, 19 November 2015, http://www.pbs.org/newshour/bb/confirming-death-france-laments-lack-of-intelligence-sharing-over-paris-suspects-movements/ (accessed 22 November 2015).

10. "At Least Two Paris Attackers 'Travelled through Greece,'" *France 24*, 21 November 2015, http://www.france24.com/en/20151121-least-two-paris-attackers-travelled-through-greece-refugees-syria-migrants (accessed 23 November 2015).

11. UNHCR, "World Refugee Day: Global Forced Displacement Tops 50 Million for First Time in Post–World War II Era," 20 June 2014, http://www.unhcr.org/53a155bc6.html (accessed 30 January 2015).

12. UNHCR, "World Refugee Day Takes Place Against a Backdrop of Worsening Global Crisis," 20 June 2015, http://www.unhcr.org/55842cb46.html (accessed 3 July 2015).

13. Merriam Webster Dictionary, "Globalization," http://www.merriam-webster.com/dictionary/globalization (accessed 29 January 2015).

14. Hans-Henrik Holm and Georg Sorenson, *Whose World Order? Uneven Globalization and the End of the Cold War* (Boulder, CO: Westview Press, 1995), 1.

15. David Harvey, cited in Nayef R. F. Al-Rodhan and Gérard Stoudmann, "Definitions of Globalization: A Comprehensive Overview and a Proposed Definition," 19 June 2006, Geneva Centre for Security Policy, http://www.wh.agh.edu.pl/other/materialy/678_2015_04_21_22_04_13_Definitions%20of%20Globalization_A%20Comprehensive%20Overview%20and%20a%20Proposed%20Definition.pdf (accessed 28 October 2015).

16. Ken'ichi Ōmae, *The Borderless World: Power and Strategy in the Global Marketplace* (London: Harper Collins, 1990).

17. David Held, et al., "Globalization," *Global Governance: A Review of Multilateralism and International Organizations* 5, no. 4 (1999): 483–484.

18. Manfred B. Steger, *Globalization: A Very Short Introduction* (Oxford: Oxford University Press, 2003), 7.

19. Immanuel Wallerstein, *World-Systems Analysis: An Introduction* (Durham, NC: Duke University Press, 2004), 93.

20. Online Etymology Dictionary, "Migration," http://etymonline.com/ (accessed 28 October 2015).

21. See, for example, Everett S. Lee, "A Theory of Migration," *Demography* 3, no. 1 (1966): 49.

22. United Nations Statistics Division, *Recommendations on Statistics of International Migration, Revision 1* (New York: United Nations, 1998), 9.

23. Chinese census data from 2000 and population sampling from 2005 indicate the number of internal migrants in China increased from 144 to 147 million. Dewen Wang, "Rural-Urban Migration and Policy in China: Challenges and Options," International Labor Organization, Asian Regional Programme on Governance of Labour Migration: Working Paper 15 (Geneva: International Labor Organization, 2008), 2.

24. United Nations Statistics Division, *Recommendations on Statistics of International Migration, Revision 1* (New York: United Nations, 1998), 10.

25. Ibid.

26. This may seem an obvious point to make, but it is important because a variety of living and nonliving things also move from one place to another. For example, animals such as birds and fish migrate, often following routes over enormous distances of thousands of miles. Plants are capable of spreading over entire continents. Planets (such as Jupiter) migrate over millions and billions of years, changing their orbits and affecting the evolution of our solar system. Even data moved from one computer to another is a form of migration.

27. Jason DeParle, "A Good Provider Is One Who Leaves," *New York Times*, 22 April 2007.

28. International Labor Organization, "Labour Migration: Facts and Figures," http://www.ilo.org/global/about-the-ilo/media-centre/issue-briefs/WCMS_239651/lang--en/index.htm (accessed 13 November 2015).

29. The Population Reference Bureau, http://www.prb.org/Publications/Reports/2013/global-migration.aspx (accessed 23 November 2015).

30. Stephen Castles cited in Ronaldo Munck, "Globalisation, Governance and Migration: An Introduction," *Third World Quarterly* 29, no. 7 (2008): 1229.

31. T. R. Malthus and Geoffrey Gilbert, *An Essay on the Principle of Population* (Oxford: Oxford University Press, 2008), 12.

32. Ibid., 17.

33. United Nations Department of Economic and Social Affairs, *World Population Prospects: The 2015 Revision* (New York: United Nations, 2015), 1.

34. This means an overwhelming number of people in the world, some 96.8 percent of the global population, did not live outside their country of origin in 2013. United Nations Department of Economic and Social Affairs, *International Migration Report 2013* (New York: United Nations, 2013), 1.

35. United Nations Department of Economic and Social Affairs, "World Population to Reach 9.6 Billion by 2050 with Most Growth in Developing Regions, Especially Africa," *World Population Prospects: The 2012 Revision, Press Release,* 13 June 2013, http://esa.un.org/unpd/wpp/Documentation/pdf/WPP2012_Press_Release.pdf (accessed 20 January 2015).

36. United Nations Department of Economic and Social Affairs, *World Population Prospects: The 2012 Revision* (New York: United Nations, 2013), 2.

37. United Nations Department of Economic and Social Affairs, "World Population to Reach 9.6 Billion by 2050," *Press Release,* 13 June 2013.

38. Lauren Frayer, "In Spain, Entire Villages Are Up For Sale—And They're Going Cheap," *NPR News,* 23 August 2015, http://www.npr.org/sections/parallels/2015/08/23/433228503/in-spain-entire-villages-are-up-for-sale-and-theyre-going-cheap (accessed 14 November 2015).

39. Lauren Frayer, "Portugal's Baby Bust Is A Stark Sign Of Hard Times," *NPR News,* 1 January 2014, http://www.npr.org/sections/parallels/2014/01/01/252068329/portugals-baby-bust-is-a-stark-sign-of-hard-times (accessed 14 November 2015).

40. For a fuller discussion see Frank J. Lechner and John Boli, "Part II: Explaining Globalization," in *The Globalization Reader* (Malden, MA: Blackwell Publishing, 2004), 53–120.

41. D. B. Grigg, "E.G. Ravenstein and the 'Laws of Migration,'" *Journal of Historical Geography* 3, no. 1 (1977): 41.

42. E. G. Ravenstein, "The Laws of Migration," *Journal of the Statistical Society of London* 48, no. 2 (1885): 167.

43. E. G. Ravenstein, "The Laws of Migration," *Journal of the Statistical Society of London* 52, no. 2 (1889): 286.

44. Ibid.

45. Everett S. Lee, "A Theory of Migration," *Demography* 3, no. 1 (1966): 48–51.

46. J. J. Mangalam and Harry K. Schwarzweller, "Some Theoretical Guidelines Toward a Sociology of Migration," *International Migration Review* 4, no. 2 (1970): 5.

47. Adrian Favell, "Rebooting Migration Theory: Interdisciplinarity, Globality and Postdisciplinarity in Migration Studies," in *Migration Theory: Talk-*

ing Across Disciplines, ed. Caroline Brettell and James Hollifield (New York: Routledge, 2008), 259–60.

48. Oscar Handlin's *The Uprooted* (Boston: Little, Brown, 1951), Marcus Lee Hansen and Arthur M. Schlesinger's *The Atlantic Migration, 1607–1860* (New York: Harper, 1940), and John Higham's *Strangers in the Land* (New Brunswick, NJ: Rutgers University Press, 2002) are written with a literary flair rarely seen today. Hansen and Handlin won the Pulitzer Prize for History in 1941 and 1952, respectively. In a similar vein, Bernard Bailyn's *Voyagers to the West* (New York: Alfred A. Knopf, 1986) won the Pulitzer Prize for History in 1987.

49. I draw on Immanuel Wallerstein's trilogy *The Modern World-System I: Capitalist Agriculture and the Origins of the European World-Economy in the Sixteenth Century* (Berkeley: University of California Press, 2011); *The Modern World-System II: Mercantilism and the Consolidation of the European World-Economy, 1600–1750* (Berkeley: University of California Press, 2011); *The Modern World-System III: The Second Era of Great Expansion of the Capitalist World-Economy, 1730–1840s* (Berkeley: University of California, 2011). For a succinct summary of these lengthy works, see Immanuel Wallerstein, *World-Systems Analysis: An Introduction* (Durham, NC: Duke University Press, 2004). The clearest explanation of the world-systems approach to migration is found in Douglas S. Massey, et al., "Contemporary Theories of International Migration," in *Worlds in Motion: Understanding International Migration at the End of the Millennium* (Oxford: Clarendon Press, 2005). See also Elizabeth McLean Petras, "The Global Labor Market in the Modern World Economy," in *Global Trends in Migration*, eds. Mary Kritz, Charles Keely, and Silvano Tomasi (New York: Center for Migration Studies, 1981), 44–63; Ewa Morawska, "Historical-Structural Models of International Migration," in *An Introduction to International Migration Studies: European Perspectives*, eds. Marco Martinello and Jan Rath (Amsterdam: Amsterdam University Press, 2012), 57–77; Alejandro Portes and John Walton, *Labor, Class, and the International System* (New York: Academic Press, 1981); and Saskia Sassen, *The Mobility of Labor and Capital: A Study in International Investment and Labor Flow* (Cambridge: Cambridge University Press, 1990).

50. Wallerstein, *World-Systems Analysis: An Introduction*, 92.

51. Saskia Sassen, *The Global City: New York, London, Tokyo* (Princeton, NJ: Princeton University Press, 2001).

52. Robert A. McLeman, *Climate and Human Migration: Past Experiences, Future Challenges* (New York: Cambridge University Press, 2014), 10.

53. B. R. Tomlinson, "What is the Third World?" *Journal of Contemporary History* 38, no. 2 (2003): 308.

54. International Organization for Migration, *World Migration Report 2013* (Geneva: International Organization for Migration, 2013), 25, 55–60. The Popu-

lation Reference Bureau, however, estimates that slightly more migration goes South to South (36 percent) than South to North (35 percent), http://www.prb .org/Publications/Reports/2013/global-migration.aspx (accessed 23 November 2015).

55. Anthony Giddens, cited in Al-Rodhan and Stoudmann, 12.

56. Ōmae, *The Borderless World*.

CHAPTER 2

1. Roger Ebert, *The Emigrants*, 15 February 1973, http://www.rogerebert .com/reviews/the-emigrants-1973 (accessed 30 October 2015).

2. Ibid.

3. Ibid.

4. Vilhelm Moberg wrote *The Emigrants* (New York: Simon & Schuster, 1951); *Unto a Good Land* (New York: Simon & Schuster, 1954); *The Settlers* (St. Paul, MN: Borealis Books, 1961); and *The Last Letter Home* (New York: Simon & Schuster, 1961). Jan Troell directed *The Emigrants* (Burbank, CA: Warner Home Video, 1994) and *The New Land* (Burbank, CA: Warner Home Video, 1994).

5. *Allt för Sverige* (Everything for Sweden), a hit reality-television show in Sweden, depicts Americans of Swedish descent who return to find their roots. The participants compete in cultural challenges for the grand prize of meeting their long-lost relatives. The show is both moving and hilarious as the likable Americans discover their cultural heritage and the striking beauty of the Old Country. It is premised on the fact that "in the years 1846–1930, 1.3 million Swedish people immigrated to America to build a better life for their families. Today, more than 4.8 million Americans have Swedish heritage," http://www .greatswedishadventure.com/; and http://www.svt.se/allt-for-sverige/ (accessed 5 November 2015).

6. Bjarni Herjólfsson may have preceded Leif Ericson. For a classic account, see T. D. Kendrick, *A History of the Vikings* (New York: Dover, 2004).

7. "The Saga of Eric the Red," in *Early America Writing,* ed. Giles Gunn (New York: Penguin Books, 1994), 23–24.

8. Ibid.

9. In 1978 the Viking settlement was designated a UNESCO World Heritage Site.

10. Christopher Columbus, "Letter to Lord Raphael Sanchez, Treasurer to Ferdinand and Isabella, King and Queen of Spain, on His First Voyage (1493)," in *Early America Writing*, ed. Giles Gunn (New York: Penguin Books, 1994), 28.

11. Columbus, "Letter to Lord Raphael Sanchez," *Early America Writing*, 31.

12. James Loewen, *Lies My Teacher Told Me* (New York: Simon & Schuster, 1995), 43.

13. Ibid.

14. Columbus, "Letter to Lord Raphael Sanchez," *Early America Writing*, 28–29.

15. Alfred Crosby, "The Columbian Exchange: Biological and Cultural Consequences of 1492," in *Readings in World Civilizations* (New York: St. Martin's Press, 1992), 29–30.

16. Noble David Cook, *Born to Die: Disease and New World Conquest, 1492–1650* (Cambridge: Cambridge University Press, 1998), 5.

17. Henry Dobyns, *Their Number Become Thinned: Native American Population Dynamics in Eastern North America* (Knoxville: University of Tennessee Press, 1983), 34; quoted in Nathan Nunn and Nancy Qian, "The Columbian Exchange: A History of Disease, Food, and Ideas," *Journal of Economic Perspectives* 24, no. 2 (2010): 163–188.

18. Jared Diamond, *Guns, Germs and Steel: The Fates of Human Societies* (New York: W. W. Norton and Co., 1997), 16.

19. William M. Denevan, *The Native Population of the Americas in 1492* (Madison: University of Wisconsin Press, 1992), xxviii.

20. Denevan, *The Native Population of the Americas in 1492*, xxvix.

21. Albert M. Craig, *The Heritage of World Civilizations* (New York: Macmillan Publishing Company, 1990), 580.

22. Karl Polanyi, *The Great Transformation: The Political and Economic Origins of Our Time* (Boston: Beacon Press, 2001), 35.

23. Mark Overton, *Agricultural Revolution in England: The Transformation of the Agrarian Economy, 1500–1850* (Cambridge: Cambridge University Press, 1996).

24. Oscar Handlin, *The Uprooted* (Boston: Little, Brown, 1990), 19.

25. For an interesting account of the Black Death in England, see Colin Platt, *King Death: The Black Death and Its Aftermath in Late-Medieval England* (Toronto: Routledge, 2001).

26. Frederick Engels, *The Condition of the Working Class in England* (London: ProQuest, 2001), 63–64.

27. Liana Ardi, "Agricultural Revolution," *Europe 1789–1914: Encyclopedia of the Age of Industry and Empire*, ed. John Merriman and Jay Winter (Detroit: Charles Scribner's Sons, 2006), 24–29.

28. Adam Smith, *The Wealth of Nations* (New York: Modern Library, 2000), 485.

29. Smith, *Wealth of Nations*, 15.

30. Engels, *Condition of the Working Class*, 83.

31. Ibid., 84.

32. "The Sadler Report of the House of Commons," in *Readings in World Civilizations: The Development of the Modern World*, Volume II, ed. Kevin Reilly (New York: St. Martin's Press, 1992), 130–134.

33. Karl Marx, "Estranged Labour," *Princeton Readings in Political Thought: Essential Texts Since Plato*, ed. Mitchell Cohen and Nicole Fermon (Princeton, NJ: Princeton University Press, 1996), 438–448.

34. Cyrus Francis Dickinson, *Dickinson Family Record* (unpublished), 21.

35. Ibid., 22.

36. Marcus Lee Hansen, *The Atlantic Migration, 1607–1860* (New York: Harper, 1961), 9.

37. Smith, *Wealth of Nations,* 675.

38. "The Declaration of Independence," http://www.archives.gov/exhibits/charters/declaration_transcript.html (accessed 5 November 2015).

39. Aristide Zolberg, *A Nation by Design: Immigration Policy in the Fashioning of America* (Cambridge, MA: Harvard University Press, 2006), 19.

40. Herman Melville cited in Zolberg, *A Nation by Design,* 455.

41. "John O'Sullivan Declares 'Boundless Future' is America's 'Manifest Destiny,'" in *Major Problems in American Immigration History*, ed. Mae Ngai and Jon Gjerde (Boston: Wadsworth, 2013), 152–153.

42. Frederick Law Olmsted, *A Journey through Texas* (New York: Mason Brothers, 1859), 502, cited in David Montejano, "Anglos Establish Control in Texas," in *Major Problems in American Immigration History*, 168.

43. "Senator Albert J. Beveridge Supports an American Empire, 1898," in *Major Problems in American Immigration History*, ed. Mae Ngai and Jon Gjerde (Boston: Wadsworth, 2013), 267.

44. "Senator Albert J. Beveridge," *Major Problems in American Immigration History*, 267.

45. "The Communist Manifesto," in *Princeton Readings in Political Thought*, ed. Mitchell Cohen and Nicole Fermon (Princeton: Princeton University Press, 1996).

46. Julius Lester and Tom Feelings, *To Be a Slave* (New York: Dial Press, 1968), 21–22.

47. "Thomas Philip, a Slave Trader, Describes the Middle Passage, 1693," in *Major Problems in American Immigration History*, 49–52.

48. Ibid.

49. Lester and Feelings, *To Be a Slave,* 53.

50. For a fuller discussion, see Paul E. Lovejoy, "The Impact of the Atlantic Slave Trade on Africa: A Review of the Literature," *Journal of African History* 30, no. 3 (1989): 365–394; Patrick Manning, "Migrations of Africans to the Americas: The Impact on Africans, Africa, and the New World," *The History Teacher* 26, no. 3 (1993): 279–296; Gregory O'Malley, "Beyond the Middle

Passage: Slave Migration from the Caribbean to North America, 1619–1807," *The William and Mary Quarterly* 66, no. 1 (2009): 125–172.

51. "Genesis 9:18–25," *The Holy Bible. Revised Standard Version Containing the Old and New Testaments* (New York: T. Nelson, 1952).

52. F. D. Lugard, *The Dual Mandate in British Tropical Africa* (London: F. Cass, 1965), 617.

53. Thomas Pakenham, *The Scramble for Africa, 1876–1912* (New York: Random House, 1991).

54. Henry M. Stanley, *Through the Dark Continent, or, The Sources of the Nile Around the Great Lakes of Equatorial Africa and Down the Livingstone River to the Atlantic Ocean*, Volume 1 (Mineola, NY: Dover Publications, 1988).

55. "General Act of the Conference of Berlin Concerning the Congo," *American Journal of International Law* 3, no. 1 (1909): 9–10.

56. "General Act of the Conference of Berlin," *American Journal of International Law*, 12–13.

57. Chapter VI of the "General Act of the Conference of Berlin" addresses the "conditions essential to be fulfilled in order that new occupations upon the coasts of the African continent may be considered as effective," 24.

58. Adam Hochschild, *King Leopold's Ghost: A Story of Greed, Terror, and Heroism in Colonial Africa* (Boston: Houghton Mifflin, 1999), 226.

59. Ibid., 227.

60. Ibid., 229–230.

61. Joseph Conrad, and Franklin Walker. *Heart of Darkness and the Secret Sharer: With an Introduction, Biographical Sketch, and a Selection of Background Materials and Commentaries by Franklin Walker* (New York: Bantam Books, 1971). *Heart of Darkness* is the basis for Francis Ford Coppola's classic 1979 Vietnam War film *Apocalypse Now*. In this adaptation, Captain Willard (played by Martin Sheen) goes up the river to kill Colonel Kurtz (Marlon Brando). The era and setting are different, but the themes of foreign domination, madness and the horror of war remain.

62. Ibid., 9.

63. Ibid., 118.

64. Ibid., 132.

65. Immanuel Wallerstein, "The Rise and Future Demise of the World Capitalist System," in *The Globalization Reader*, ed. Frank Lechner and John Boli (Malden, MA: Blackwell Publishing, 2004), 67.

66. Hochschild, *King Leopold's Ghost*, 300–301.

67. "Chronicle of Death Ignored: Five Million People Have Died in Congo in a War That No One Really Understands," *The Economist*, 28 April 2011, http://www.economist.com/node/18617876 (accessed 19 November 2015).

68. Frederic Rosengarten, *Freebooters Must Die! The Life and Death of William Walker, the Most Notorious Filibuster of the Nineteenth Century* (Wayne, PA: Haverford House, 1976).

69. "Walker, William (1824–1860)," *Encyclopedia of Latin American History and Culture*, ed. Jay Kinsbruner and Erick D. Langer (Detroit: Charles Scribner's Sons, 2008), 407–408.

70. "Sandino, Augusto César (1895–1934)," *Encyclopedia of Latin American History and Culture*, 709–711.

71. "Somoza Garcia, Anastasio (1896–1956)," *Encyclopedia of Latin American History and Culture*, 894–897.

72. Holly Sklar, *Washington's War on Nicaragua* (Boston: South End Press, 1988), 7.

73. According to the television show's website, "North also serves as the honorary chairman of Freedom Alliance, the conservative public policy organization he founded in 1990 . . . The organization is dedicated to the maintenance of a strong national defense, the protection of the rights and freedoms of individual citizens, and the adoption of policies that promote free enterprise," http://www.foxnews.com/person/n/oliver-north.html (accessed 28 November 2015).

74. Duncan Campbell, "Philip Agee: The Man Who Blew the Whistle on the CIA's Backing of Military Dictatorships," 10 January 2008 http://www.theguardian.com/news/2008/jan/10/mainsection.duncancampbell (accessed 22 November 2015).

75. Philip Agee, *Inside the Company: CIA Diary* (Harmondsworth: Penguin, 1975), 517.

76. Loewen, *Lies My Teacher Told Me*, 42–43.

CHAPTER 3

1. Sonia Nazario, "Chapter One: The Boy Left Behind," *Los Angeles Times*, 29 September 2002; Sonia Nazario, *Enrique's Journey* (New York: Random House, 2007).

2. Don Bartletti, "14 Years Later: Looking Back on a Child Migrant's Journey North on 'The Beast,'" *Los Angeles Times*, 22 August 2014.

3. Marc Rosenblum, "Unaccompanied Child Migration to the United States: The Tension between Protection and Prevention," Migration Policy Institute, April 2015, http://www.migrationpolicy.org/research/unaccompanied-child-migration-united-states-tension-between-protection-and-prevention (accessed 8 November 2015).

4. Diana Washington Valdez, "'La Bestia'—Honduran Immigrants in El Paso Describe Journey on Notorious Train," *El Paso Times*, 18 May 2014,

http://www.elpasotimes.com/news/ci_25788970/la-bestia-mdash-honduran-immigrants-el-paso-describe (accessed 8 November 2015).

5. Bartletti, "14 Years Later," *Los Angeles Times*, 22 August 2014.

6. For an overview see Douglas S. Massey, et al., "Contemporary Theories of International Migration," in *Worlds in Motion: Understanding International Migration at the End of the Millennium* (Oxford: Oxford University Press, 2005), 17–59; Russell King, "Theories and Typologies of Migration: An Overview and a Primer," Willy Brandt Series of Working Papers in International Migration and Ethnic Relations, Malmö Institute for Studies of Migration, Diversity and Welfare, 2012.

7. "Mexico," CIA World Factbook, https://www.cia.gov/library/publications/the-world-factbook/geos/mx.html (accessed 8 November 2015).

8. Sierra Stoney and Jeanne Batalova, "Mexican Immigrants in the United States," Migration Policy Institute, 28 February 2015, http://www.migrationpolicy.org/article/mexican-immigrants-united-states-2 (accessed 8 November 2015).

9. Eduardo Galeano, *Open Veins of Latin America: Five Centuries of the Pillage of a Continent* (New York: Monthly Review Press, 1973).

10. "The Official Bracero Agreement," 4 August 1942, http://www.farmworkers.org/bpaccord.html (accessed 8 November 2015).

11. Ronald Young, "Bracero Program," *St. James Encyclopedia of Labor History Worldwide*, ed. Neil Schlager (Detroit: St. James Press, 2004), 97–100.

12. Celestino Fernandez and James E. Officer, "The Lighter Side of Mexican Immigration: Humor and Satire in the Mexican Corrido," *Journal of the Southwest* 31, no. 4 (1989), 477–478.

13. Lynnaire M. Sheridan, *"I Know It's Dangerous": Why Mexicans Risk Their Lives to Cross the Border* (Tucson: University of Arizona Press, 2009), 154.

14. David Held, "Globalization," *Global Governance: A Review of Multilateralism and International Organizations* 5, no. 4 (1999), 483–484.

15. Sam Gindin and Leo Panitch, *The Making of Global Capitalism: The Political Economy of American Empire* (London: Verso, 2012), 17.

16. "Preamble," North American Free Trade Agreement, https://www.nafta-sec-alena.org/Home/Legal-Texts/North-American-Free-Trade-Agreement (accessed 8 November 2015).

17. Jen Soriano, "Globalization and the Maquiladoras," *Government, Politics, and Protest: Essential Primary Sources*, ed. K. Lee Lerner, Brenda Wilmoth Lerner, and Adrienne Wilmoth Lerner (Detroit: Gale, 2006), 356–358.

18. Soriano, "Globalization and the Maquiladoras," 356–358.

19. Timothy A. Wise, Hilda Salazar, and Laura Carlsen, "Lessons Learned: Civil Society Strategies in the Face of Economic Integration," in *Confronting*

Globalization: Economic Integration and Popular Resistance in Mexico, ed. Timothy A. Wise, Hilda Salazar, and Laura Carlson (Bloomfield, CT: Kumarian Press, 2003), 215, 223–224.

20. Jonathan Fox, "Foreword," in *Confronting Globalization: Economic Integration and Popular Resistance in Mexico*, ed. Timothy A. Wise, Hilda Salazar, and Laura Carlson (Bloomfield, CT: Kumarian Press, 2003), ix.

21. Roderic Ai Camp, "Madrid Hurtado, Miguel de la (1934–)," *Encyclopedia of Latin American History and Culture*, ed. Jay Kinsbruner and Erick D. Langer (Detroit: Charles Scribner's Sons, 2008), 319–320.

22. Roderic Ai Camp, "Salinas de Gortari, Carlos (1948–)," *Encyclopedia of Latin American History and Culture*, 679–681.

23. Roderic Ai Camp, "Zedillo Ponce de León, Ernesto (1951–)," *Encyclopedia of Latin American History and Culture*, 512–514.

24. Froylán Enciso, "Fox Quesada, Vicente (1942–)," *Encyclopedia of Latin American History and Culture*, ed. Jay Kinsbruner and Erick D. Langer (Detroit: Charles Scribner's Sons, 2008), 295–297.

25. Immanuel Wallerstein, "The Rise and Future Demise of the World Capitalist System," in *The Globalization Reader*, ed. Frank Lechner and John Boli (Malden, MA: Blackwell Publishing), 68.

26. "Mexico's Minimum Wage: Stingy by Any Measure," *The Economist*, 14 August 2014, http://www.economist.com/news/finance-and-economics/21612255-name-curbing-inflation-government-hurting-workers-stingy-any (accessed 8 November 2015); see also data from the World Bank, http://databank.worldbank.org/data//reports.aspx?source=2&country=MEX&series=&period= (accessed 8 November 2015); and CIA World Factbook, https://www.cia.gov/library/publications/the-world-factbook/geos/mx.html (accessed 8 November 2015).

27. Juan Montes, "Mexico Looks to Raise Wages," *Wall Street Journal*, 28 August 2014.

28. CIA World Factbook, https://www.cia.gov/library/publications/the-world-factbook/geos/gt.html (accessed 8 November 2015).

29. UNICEF, "UNICEF Annual Report for Guatemala 2010," http://www.unicef.org/guatemala/english/overview_18012.htm (accessed 8 November 2015).

30. Lawrence A. Yates, "Counterinsurgency," *Encyclopedia of Latin American History and Culture*, ed. Jay Kinsbruner and Erick D. Langer (Detroit: Charles Scribner's Sons, 2008), 646–647.

31. Lianne Milton, "'Life Is Worth Nothing in Guatemala,'" *Newsweek*, 2 December 2013, http://www.newsweek.com/life-worth-nothing-guatemala-207586 (accessed 5 December 2015).

32. The preceding three quotes are from Talea Miller, "Mexico Drug Cartels Moving in on Guatemala Routes," *PBS Newshour*, 15 March 2011, http://

www.pbs.org/newshour/updates/latin_america-jan-june11-drugs_03-15/ (accessed 5 December 2015).

33. David Huey, "The US War on Drugs and Its Legacy in Latin America," *The Guardian*, 3 February 2014, http://www.theguardian.com/global-development-professionals-network/2014/feb/03/us-war-on-drugs-impact-in-latin-american (accessed 14 January 2016).

34. Jamie Doward, "'War on Drugs' Has Failed, Say Latin American Leaders," *The Guardian*, 7 April 2012, http://www.theguardian.com/world/2012/apr/07/war-drugs-latin-american-leaders (accessed 14 January 2016).

35. "What America's Users Spend on Illegal Drugs: 2000–2010," Rand Corporation, February 2014, https://www.whitehouse.gov/sites/default/files/ondcp/policy-and-research/wausid_results_report.pdf (accessed 14 January 2016).

36. Ed Vulliamy, "Global Banks Are the Financial Services Wing of the Drug Cartels," *The Guardian*, 21 July 2012, http://www.theguardian.com/world/2012/jul/21/drug-cartels-banks-hsbc-money-laundering (accessed 14 January 2016).

37. Otto Pérez Molina, "Comment: In Latin America, We Know Who Is to Blame for Our Child Migrant Crisis," *The Guardian*, 3 August 2014, http://www.theguardian.com/commentisfree/2014/aug/03/child-migrants-to-us-guatamalan-president-on-human-rights-action-on-traffickers (accessed 14 January 2016).

38. "Full Interview with Former Honduras Pres. Manuel Zelaya, Ousted in U.S.-Backed Coup," *Democracy Now!* 29 July 2015, http://www.democracynow.org/blog/2015/7/29/video_full_interview_with_former_honduras# (accessed 8 November 2015).

39. Zachary Toillion, "Clinton Implicated in Honduran Coup, Emails Show," *Tennessee Star Journal*, 16 July 2015, http://tnsjournal.com/international/clinton-implicated-in-honduran-coup-emails-show/ (accessed 8 November 2015).

40. "'Blackout' Imposed as George W. Bush Speaks at Cayman Islands Investment Conference," *NBC News*, 2 November 2012, http://worldnews.nbcnews.com/_news/2012/11/02/14875519-blackout-imposed-as-george-w-bush-speaks-at-cayman-islands-investment-conference (accessed 27 November 2015).

41. Devin Dwyer, "Obama Warns Central Americans: 'Do Not Send Your Children to the Borders,'" *ABC News*, http://abcnews.go.com/Politics/obama-warns-central-americans-send-children-borders/story?id=24320063 (accessed 27 November 2015).

42. Christopher Gunness, "UNRWA: Crisis in ISIL-Controlled Palestinian Refugee Camp 'Beyond Inhumane,'" *Democracy Now!* http://www.democracynow.org/2015/4/7/headlines#471 (accessed 8 November 2015).

43. UNHCR, "Worsening Conditions Inside Syria and the Region Fuel Despair, Driving Thousands Towards Europe," 8 September 2015, http://www.unhcr.org/55eed5d66.html (accessed 8 November 2015).

44. Ibid.

45. Ibid.

46. United Nations Office for the Coordination of Humanitarian Affairs, "About the Crisis," February 2016, http://www.unocha.org/syrian-arab-republic/syria-country-profile/about-crisis (accessed 13 March 2016); Syrian Observatory for Human Rights, "More than 55,000 Killed in Syria in 2015," 2 January 2016, http://www.syriahr.com/en/?p=41912 (accessed 13 March 2016); Anne Barnard, "Death Toll From War in Syria Now 470,000, Group Finds," 11 February 2016, *New York Times*, http://www.nytimes.com/2016/02/12/world/middleeast/death-toll-from-war-in-syria-now-470000-group-finds.html?_r=0 (accessed 13 March 2016).

47. Anne Barnard and Karam Shoumali, "Image of Drowned Syrian, Aylan Kurdi, 3, Brings Migrant Crisis into Focus," *New York Times*, 3 September 2015.

48. UNHCR, "Syria Regional Refugee Response," http://data.unhcr.org/syrianrefugees/regional.php (accessed 8 November 2015).

49. "Germany Raises Estimate on Refugee Arrivals to 800,000 This Year," 20 August 2015, *The Guardian*, http://www.theguardian.com/world/2015/aug/20/germany-raises-estimate-refugee-arrivals-800000 (accessed 8 November 2015).

50. Felicity Capon, "Germany Now Expects Up to 1.5 Million Asylum Seekers in 2015: Report," *Newsweek*, 5 October 2015, http://europe.newsweek.com/germany-now-expects-1-5-million-asylum-seekers-2015-report-334107 (accessed 25 November 2015).

51. "German Lawmaker: At the Root of Refugee Crisis are Wars Led by the United States in the Middle East," *Democracy Now!* 9 September 2015, http://www.democracynow.org/2015/9/9/german_lawmaker_at_the_root_of (accessed 8 November 2015).

52. Ed O'Keefe, "Jeb Bush Touts Familiar Worldview to a Wary Public," *The Washington Post*, 17 April 2015.

53. Stated as a hypothesis: "Political and military interventions by governments of capitalist countries to protect investments abroad and to support foreign governments, when they fail, produce refugee movements directed to particular core countries, constituting another form of international migration." Douglas Massey, et al., *Worlds in Motion* (New York: Clarendon Press, 2008), 41.

54. Macer Hall, "Gaddafi's £4BN Migrant Demand," in *Introducing Globalization*, ed. Richard Mansbach and Edward Rhodes (Washington, D.C.: CQ Press, 2013), 184–185.

55. "Gaddafi Wants EU Cash to Stop African Migrants," *British Broadcasting Corporation*, 31 August 2010, http://www.bbc.com/news/world-eu rope-11139345 (accessed 8 November 2015).

56. Human Rights Watch, "Death of Dictator: Bloody Vengeance in Sirte," 16 October 2012, https://www.hrw.org/report/2012/10/16/death-dictator/ bloody-vengeance-sirte (accessed 8 November 2015).

57. International Organization for Migration (IOM), "Migrant Arrivals by Sea in Italy Top 170,000 in 2014," 16 January 2015, https://www.iom .int/news/migrant-arrivals-sea-italy-top-170000-2014 (accessed 8 November 2015).

58. Nick Squires, "Migrants Tell of Deepening Chaos in Libya: Everyone Is Armed Now," *The Telegraph,* 22 February 2015, http://www.telegraph.co.uk/ news/worldnews/africaandindianocean/libya/11427306/Migrants-tell-of-deep ening-chaos-in-Libya-Everyone-is-armed-now.html (accessed 8 November 2015).

59. Nick Squires, "The Shocking Abuse Refugees Endure at the Hands of People Smugglers in Libya," *The Telegraph,* 22 February 2015, http://www .telegraph.co.ukws/worldnews/africaandindianocean/libya/11428572/The- shocking-abuse-refugees-endure-at-the-hands-of-people-smugglers-in-Libya. html (accessed 8 November 2015).

60. David D. Kirkpatrick, "From Lawless Libya to the Sea," *New York Times,* 11 May 2015.

61. Tim Appenzeller and Dennis R. Dimick, "Global Warming: Bulletins from a Warmer World," *National Geographic* 206, no. 3 (2004): 2–75.

62. Naomi Klein, *This Changes Everything: Capitalism vs. The Climate* (New York: Simon & Schuster, 2014), 18.

63. Jared Diamond, *Collapse: How Societies Choose to Fail or Succeed* (New York: Viking, 2005), 508.

64. "Bangladesh," CIA World Factbook, https://www.cia.gov/library/pub lications/the-world-factbook/geos/bg.html (accessed 8 November 2015).

65. National Oceanic and Atmospheric Administration, "NOAA's Top Global Weather, Water and Climate Events of the Twentieth Century," 13 December 1999, http://www.noaanews.noaa.gov/stories/images/global.pdf (ac cessed 8 November 2015).

66. Koko Warner, et al., *In Search of Shelter: Mapping the Effects of Climate Change on Human Migration and Displacement* (Bonn: United Nations Univer sity Institute for Environment and Human Security, 2009), 13.

67. Warner, et al., *In Search of Shelter,* 13.

68. Gardiner Harris, "As Seas Rise, Millions Cling to Borrowed Time and Dying Land," *New York Times,* 29 March 2014.

69. Ibid.

70. Ibid.

71. OECD, "What Are the Social Benefits of Education?" *Education Indicators in Focus* (Paris: OECD Publishing, 2014), http://dx.doi.org/10.1787/5k4ddxnl39vk-en (accessed 8 November 2015).

72. Karl Polanyi quoted in John Gray, "From the Great Transformation to the Global Free Market," ed. Frank Lechner and John Boli (Malden, MA: Blackwell Publishing), 22.

CHAPTER 4

1. Ayaan Hirsi Ali, *Nomad: A Personal Journey Through the Clash of Civilizations* (Toronto: A. A. Knopf Canada, 2010), xiii.

2. Ibid., xv.

3. Jane Kramer, "The Dutch Model: Multiculturalism and Muslim Immigrants," *The New Yorker*, 3 April 2006, 60–67.

4. Jackie Smith, et al., *Global Democracy and the World Social Forums* (Boulder, CO: Paradigm Publishers, 2008), 53.

5. International Organization for Migration, *World Migration Report 2013* (Geneva: International Organization for Migration), 25.

6. "Enoch Powell's 'Rivers of Blood Speech,'" *The Telegraph*, 6 November 2007, http://www.telegraph.co.uk/comment/3643823/Enoch-Powells-Rivers-of-Blood-speech.html (accessed 9 November 2015).

7. Ibid.

8. Zig Layton-Henry, "Britain: From Immigration Control to Migration Management," in *Controlling Immigration: A Global Perspective*, ed. Wayne A. Cornelius, et al. (Stanford: Stanford University Press, 2004).

9. Simon Cottee, "'I Am Strange Here': Conversations With the Syrians in Calais," *The Atlantic*, 17 August 2015, http://www.theatlantic.com/international/archive/2015/08/calais-migrant-camp-uk-syria/401459/ (accessed 9 November 2015).

10. For a classic analysis, see Rogers Brubaker, *Citizenship and Nationhood in France and Germany* (Cambridge, MA: Harvard University Press, 1992). For a thorough comparative study, see Martin Schain, *The Politics of Immigration in France, Britain, and the United States: A Comparative Study* (New York: Palgrave Macmillan, 2008).

11. Timothy Christenfeld, "The World: Alien Expressions; Wretched Refuse is Just the Start," *New York Times*, 10 March 1996.

12. "Le Pen Compares Migrant Influx to Barbarian Invasion of Rome," *Reuters News Agency*, 15 September 2015, https://www.rt.com/news/315466-le-pen-migrant-barbarian-invasion/ (accessed 9 November 2015).

13. Max Frisch, *Gesammelte Werke in zeitlicher Folge: Band V* (Frankfurt am Main: Suhrkamp, 1976), 374.

14. "Basic Law for the Federal Republic of Germany," https://www.btg-bestellservice.de/pdf/80201000.pdf (accessed 9 November 2015).

15. For a fuller discussion, see Eliot Dickinson, "Citizenship in the Federal Republic of Germany," *Humanities and Social Sciences Review* 3, no. 2 (2014): 155–171; Eliot Dickinson, "The Federal Republic of Germany: Immigration and National Identity," in *History (1933–1948): What We Choose to Remember*, ed. Margaret Monahan Hogan and James M. Lies, C.S.C. (Portland, OR: University of Portland, 2011), 329–353.

16. Carlo Angerer and Claudio Lavanga, "Hungary Refugees Begin 300-Mile Walk to Germany Amid Train Impasse," *NBC News*, 4 September 2015, http://www.nbcnews.com/news/world/migrants-budapest-hungary-refuse-leave-camp-bound-train-n421601 (accessed 9 November 2015).

17. The number of asylum applications fluctuated during this period; there were 10,050 in 2010, 40,360 in 2011, 17,350 in 2012, 25,720 in 2013, and 63,660 in 2014. UNHCR, *Asylum Trends 2014* (Geneva: UNHCR, 2015), 20.

18. UNHCR, "The Sea Route to Europe: The Mediterranean Passage in the Age of Refugees," 1 July 2015, http://www.unhcr.org/5592b9b36.html (accessed 9 November 2015).

19. UNHCR, "UNHCR Shocked as Boat Tragedy Leaves Scores Dead Off Italian Coast," 3 October 2013, http://www.unhcr.org/524d4ab36.html (accessed 9 November 2015).

20. UNHCR, "UNHCR Chief expresses shock at new Mediterranean boat tragedy," 12 October 2013, http://www.unhcr.org/52594c6a6.html (accessed 9 November 2015).

21. Ministero della Difesa, "Mare Nostrum Operation," http://www.marina.difesa.it/EN/operations/Pagine/MareNostrum.aspx (accessed 9 November 2015).

22. IOM, "IOM Assists Probes into the Deaths of Hundreds of Migrants Lost this Month Off the Coast of Malta," 23 September 2014, https://www.iom.int/cms/en/sites/iom/home/news-and-views/press-briefing-notes/pbn-2014b/pbn-listing/iom-assists-probes-into-the-deat.html (accessed 9 November 2015).

23. UNHCR, "UNHCR Alarmed at Death Toll from Boat Sinkings in Mediterranean," 16 September 2014, http://www.unhcr.org/54184ae76.html (accessed 9 November 2015).

24. Dominik Straub, "Italiens Kosten für Flüchtlinge steigen," 27 April 2015, http://derstandard.at/2000014947246/Italiens-Kosten-fuer-Fluechtlinge-steigen (accessed 9 November 2015).

25. Alan Travis, "UK Axes Support for Mediterranean Migrant Rescue Operation," *The Guardian*, 27 October 2014, http://www.theguardian.com/politics/2014/oct/27/uk-mediterranean-migrant-rescue-plan (accessed 9 November 2015).

26. For the full written question-and-answer exchange, see the United Kingdom Parliament, Written Answers, 15 October 2014, http://www.publications.parliament.uk/pa/ld201415/ldhansrd/text/141015w0001.htm (accessed 9 November 2015).

27. Travis, "UK Axes Support."

28. UNHCR, "Mediterranean Crossings More Deadly a Year After Lampedusa Tragedy," 2 October 2014, http://www.unhcr.org/print/542d12de9.html (accessed 9 November 2015).

29. UNHCR, "Update: Major Tragedy in the Mediterranean Confirmed, 300 Migrants and Refugees Are Missing," 11 February 2015, http://www.unhcr.org/54db3dd69.html (accessed 9 November 2015).

30. UNHCR, "UNHCR Shock at Latest Deaths on Mediterranean, Rescue Capacity Needed More Urgently Than Ever," 15 April 2015, http://www.unhcr.org/552e54cf9.html (accessed 9 November 2015).

31. Most estimates of the number of fatalities in the 19 April shipwreck range from 700 to 900. UNHCR, "UNHCR—New Mediterranean Boat Tragedy May Be Biggest Ever, Urgent Action Is Needed Now," 19 April 2015, http://www.unhcr.org/5533c2406.html (accessed 9 November 2015).

32. UNHCR, "UNHCR Welcomes EU Mediterranean Plans, but Says More Needs to Be Done," 21 April 2015, http://www.unhcr.org/553623109.html (accessed 9 November 2015).

33. European Commission, "A European Agenda on Migration," 13 May 2015.

34. European Commission, "Press Release: Managing Migration Better," 13 May 2015.

35. Ibid.

36. Hellenic Statistical Authority, "2011 Population and Housing Census: Migration," http://www.statistics.gr/portal/page/portal/ESYE/PAGE-census2011 (accessed 9 November 2015). See also Charalambos Kasimis, "Greece: Illegal Immigration in the Midst of Crisis," Migration Policy Institute, 8 March 2012, http://www.migrationpolicy.org/article/greece-illegal-immigration-midst-crisis (accessed 9 November 2015).

37. European Union Court of Justice, "An Asylum Seeker May Not Be Transferred to a Member State Where He Risks Being Subjected to Inhuman Treatment," Press Release No. 140/11, 21 December 2011.

38. Nathalie Savaricas, "Greece Plan to Release 3,500 Immigrants from Asylum Centres Sets it on a Collision Course with Europe," *The Independent*,

5 April 2015, http://www.independent.co.uk/news/world/europe/greece-plan-to-release-3500-illegal-immigrants-from-asylum-centres-sets-it-on-a-collision-course-with-europe-10157380.html (accessed 9 November 2015).

39. Helena Smith, "Migrants Face 'Living Hell' in Greek Detention," *The Guardian*, 1 April 2014, http://www.theguardian.com/world/2014/apr/01/migrants-living-hell-greek-detention-medecins-sans-frontieres-scabies-tb (accessed 9 November 2015).

40. Doctors Without Borders, "Invisible Suffering," 1 April 2014, http://www.doctorswithoutborders.org/news-stories/special-report/invisible-suffering-migrants-detained-greece (accessed 9 November 2015).

41. Hellenic Statistical Authority, *Greece in Figures 2014* (Piraeus: Statistical Information and Publications Division, 2014), 6–7.

42. Charles C. Branas, et al., "The Impact of Economic Austerity and Prosperity Events on Suicide in Greece: A 30-year Interrupted Time-series Analysis," *BMJ Open*, 2 February 2015, http://bmjopen.bmj.com/content/5/1/e005619.full.pdf+html (accessed 9 November 2015).

43. Nikolia Apostolou, "Flood of Migrants Besets Greece," *The Washington Times*, 3 December 2014, http://www.washingtontimes.com/news/2014/dec/3/syrian-refugees-flood-greek-shores/?page=all (accessed 9 November 2015).

44. "Greece," European Commission Economic and Financial Affairs, http://ec.europa.eu/economy_finance/eu/countries/greece_en.htm (accessed 9 November 2015).

45. Conor Gaffey, "Greece Backtracks Over Threat to Send Jihadist Refugees to Germany," *Newsweek*, 13 March 2014, http://europe.newsweek.com/greece-backtracks-over-threat-send-jihadist-refugees-germany-313717 (accessed 9 November 2015).

46. Inés Benítez, "Sea Swallows the Stories of Africans Drowned at Ceuta," *Inter Press Service News Agency*, 10 March 2014, http://www.ipsnews.net/2014/03/sea-swallows-stories-africans-drowned-ceuta/ (accessed 9 November 2015).

47. UNHCR, "UNHCR Concerned Over Spain's Bid to Legalize Push-backs From Enclaves," 28 October 2014, http://www.unhcr.org/print/544f7c669.html (accessed March 18, 2015).

48. Ashifa Kassam, "Morocco Destroys Migrant Camps Near Border with Spanish Enclave," *The Guardian*, 11 February 2015, http://www.theguardian.com/world/2015/feb/11/morocco-destroys-migrant-camps-melilla-spain-border (accessed 9 November 2015).

49. UNHCR, "UNHCR Concerned Over Spain's Bid to Legalize Push-backs From Enclaves," 28 October 2014.

50. "Storming a Spanish Border in North Africa," *New York Times*, 30 May 2014.

51. "Europe's High Tech Fortress," *Der Spiegel*, 8 October 2011.

52. Ayuba's story is described in detail in an article by Yassin Musharbash, "Assaulting Ceuta and Melilla: Through the Razor Wire and into the EU," *Der Spiegel*, 10 March 2005, http://www.spiegel.de/international/assaulting-ceuta-and-melilla-through-the-razor-wire-and-into-the-eu-a-377783.html (accessed 9 November 2015).

53. Raphael Minder, "Memo From Melilla: At Spanish Enclave, a Debate Over What Makes a Border," *New York Times*, 24 November 2014.

54. "GDP Per Capita (Current US$)," *The World Bank*, http://data.world bank.org/indicator/NY.GDP.PCAP.CD (accessed 10 November 2015).

55. Spain's unemployment more than tripled from 8.2 percent in 2007 to 26.1 percent in 2013; by contrast, Germany's dropped from 8.7 percent to 5.3 percent in the same time period. Eurostat, http://ec.europa.eu/eurostat/statistics-explained/images/7/77/Unemployment_rate%2C_2002-2013_%28%25%29.png (accessed November 2015).

56. George Stolz, "Europe's Back Doors," *The Atlantic,* January 2000.

57. "It Costs $10,000 to Get from A to B. Even if B is the Seabed," *The Guardian*, 21 October 2014.

58. Minder, "Memo From Melilla," *New York Times*.

59. See Ashifa Kassam, "African Migrants Look Down on White-clad Golfers in Viral Photo," *The Guardian*, 23 October 2014, http://www.theguardian.com/world/2014/oct/23/-sp-african-migrants-look-down-on-white-clad-golf ers-in-viral-photo (accessed 9 March 2016); David Sim, "Spain: Photo of Golfers in Melilla and African Migrants Clinging to Border Fence Goes Viral," *International Business Times*, 23 October 2014, http://www.ibtimes.co.uk/spain-photo-golfers-melilla-african-migrants-clinging-border-fence-goes-viral-1471496 (accessed 9 March 2016).

60. "Preamble," *Treaty of Rome*, 25 March 1957, http://ec.europa.eu/archives/emu_history/documents/treaties/rometreaty2.pdf (accessed 10 November 2015).

61. "Article 8A," *Single European Act*, 1 July 1987, http://eur-lex.europa.eu/legal-content/EN/TXT/?uri=uriserv:xy0027 (accessed 10 November 2015).

62. "Part Two: Citizenship of the Union, Article 8a," *Maastricht Treaty on European Union* (Luxembourg: Office for Official Publications of the European Communities, 1992).

63. European Commission, *Europe of Free Movement: The Schengen Area* (Brussels: Home Affairs Publications Office, 2011), 3.

64. International Physicians for the Prevention of Nuclear War, "Body Count: Casualty Figures after 10 Years of the 'War on Terror,'" March 2015, http://www.psr.org/resources/body-count.html (accessed 10 November 2015).

65. Council of European Union, *The Schengen Acquis: Integrated into the European Union* (Luxembourg: Office for Official Publications of the European Communities, 2001), 95.

66. Marina Koren, "How the Paris Attacks Are Changing the EU's Debate on Refugees," *The Atlantic*, 16 November 2015, http://www.theatlantic.com/international/archive/2015/11/paris-attack-refugees/416175/ (accessed 30 November 2015).

67. Ian Traynor, "Europe Split over Refugee Deal as Germany Leads Breakaway Coalition," *The Guardian*, 30 November 2015, http://www.theguardian.com/world/2015/nov/29/germanys-plan-to-strike-eu-wide-refugee-sharing-deal-stalls (accessed 30 November 2015).

68. Peter Cluskey, "Dutch PM Proposes 'Mini Schengen' Amid Calls for New Fortress Europe," *The Irish Times*, 27 November 2015, http://www.irishtimes.com/news/world/europe/dutch-pm-proposes-mini-schengen-amid-calls-for-new-fortress-europe-1.2446480 (accessed 30 November 2015).

69. Juliane von Mittelstaedt and Maximilian Popp, "'Aren't We Human Beings?': One Year after the Lampedusa Refugee Tragedy," *Der Spiegel Online*, 10 September 2014, http://www.spiegel.de/international/europe/lampedusa-survivors-one-year-after-the-refugee-tragedy-a-994887.html (accessed 30 November 2015).

70. European Commission, "Public Opinion in the European Union," *Standard Eurobarometer* 82, (Autumn 2014): 33.

71. European Commission, "Public Opinion in the European Union," *Standard Eurobarometer* 83, (Autumn 2015): 14.

72. "Charter of Fundamental Rights of the European Union," http://eur-lex.europa.eu/legal-content/EN/TXT/?uri=CELEX:12012P/TXT (accessed 30 November 2015).

73. Manuel Castells, *The Informational City: Information Technology, Economic Restructuring, and the Urban-Regional Process* (Oxford: Blackwell, 1989), 1.

74. Jagdish Bhagwati, "Borders Beyond Control," *Foreign Affairs* 82, no. 1 (2003): 98–104.

75. Jere R. Behrman and Nevzer Stacey, *The Social Benefits of Education* (Ann Arbor: University of Michigan Press, 1997).

76. Stephen Moore, "Give Us Your Best, Your Brightest: Immigration Policy Benefits Society Despite Increasing Problems," in Anthony Messina and Gallya Lahav, *The Migration Reader: Exploring Politics and Policy* (Boulder, CO: Lynne Rienner Publishers, 2006), 329–333.

77. Frédéric Docquier and Hillel Rapoport, "Globalization, Brain Drain, and Development," *Journal of Economic Literature* 50, no. 3 (2012): 725.

78. Çaglar Özden, "Educated Migrants: Is There Brain Waste?" in Çaglar Özden and Maurice W. Schiff, *International Migration, Remittances, and the Brain Drain* (Washington, D.C.: World Bank, 2006), 227–244.

79. Jennifer A. Kingson, "Alaska, Oregon or . . . Detroit?" *New York Times*, 23 September 2014.

80. Ibid.

81. UNHCR, "In search of shelter: Mapping the effects of climate change on human migration and displacement," http://mtnforum.org/content/search-shelter-mapping-effects-climate-change-human-migration-and-displacement (accessed 10 November 2015).

82. UNHCR, *States Parties to the 1951 Convention Relating to the Status of Refugees and the 1967 Protocol*, http://www.unhcr.org/3b73b0d63.html (accessed 10 November 2015).

83. Karl Marx and Friedrich Engels, "The Communist Manifesto," in Mitchell Cohen and Nicole Fermon, *Princeton Readings in Political Thought: Essential Texts Since Plato* (Princeton, NJ: Princeton University Press, 1996), 448–463. This excerpt is, arguably, an imperfect rendering of the original German: *Alle festen eingerosteten Verhältnisse mit ihrem Gefolge von altehrwürdigen Vorstellungen und Anschauungen werden aufgelöst, alle neugebildeten veralten, ehe sie verknöchern können. Alles Ständische und Stehende verdampft, alles Heilige wird entweiht, und die Menschen sind endlich gezwungen, ihre Lebensstellung, ihre gegenseitigen Beziehungen mit nüchternen Augen anzusehen.* Discerning readers may prefer the following translation: "All the settled, age-old relations with their train of time-honoured preconceptions and viewpoints are dissolved; all newly formed ones become outmoded before they can ossify. Everything feudal and fixed goes up in smoke, everything sacred is profaned, and men are finally forced to take a down-to-earth view of their circumstances, their multifarious relationships." Karl Marx and Terrell Carver, *Marx: Later Political Writings* (Cambridge: Cambridge University Press, 1996), 4.

CHAPTER 5

1. Emma O'Brien, "An Islander's Bid to Be the World's First Climate Refugee," *Bloomberg Business*, 30 March 2015.

2. Amy Maas, "Tuvalu Climate Change Family Win NZ Residency Appeal," *The New Zealand Herald*, 3 August 2014.

3. Immigration and Protection Tribunal New Zealand, "Decision," Auckland, 4 June 2014, NZIPT 501370-371, https://forms.justice.govt.nz/search/IPT/Documents/Deportation/pdf/rem_20140604_501370.pdf (accessed 30 October 2015).

4. Ibid.

5. Rick Noack, "Has the Era of the 'Climate Change Refugee' Begun?" *Washington Post*, 7 August 2014.

6. Oliver Balch, "The Pacific Islands: Tomorrow's Climate Refugees Struggle to Access Water Today," *The Guardian*, 25 February 2015.

7. Kennedy Warne, "Will Pacific Island Nations Disappear as Seas Rise? Maybe Not: Reef Islands Can Grow and Change as Sediments Shift, Studies Show," *National Geographic*, 13 February 2015, http://news.nation algeographic.com/2015/02/150213-tuvalu-sopoaga-kench-kiribati-maldives-cyclone-marshall-islands/ (accessed 30 October 2015).

8. "Encyclical Letter *Laudato Si'* of the Holy Father Francis on Care for our Common Home," http://w2.vatican.va/content/francesco/en/encyclicals/documents/papa-francesco_20150524_enciclica-laudato-si.html (accessed 10 November 2015); Anthony Faiola and Michael Birnbaum, "Pope Calls on Europe's Catholics to Take in refugees," *Washington Post*, 6 September 2015, https://www.washingtonpost.com/world/refugees-keep-streaming-into-europe-as-crisis-continues-unabated/2015/09/06/8a330572-5345-11e5-b225-90edbd49f362_story.html (accessed 10 November 2015).

9. Michael Roskin, *Countries and Concepts: An Introduction to Comparative Politics*, 6th edition, (Upper Saddle River, NJ: Prentice Hall, 1998), p. xxi.

10. "Full Text: Donald Trump Announces a Presidential Bid," *Washington Post*, 16 June 2015, http://www.washingtonpost.com/news/post-politics/wp/2015/06/16/full-text-donald-trump-announces-a-presidential-bid/# (accessed 30 October 2015).

11. "Full Text: Donald Trump Announces a Presidential Bid," *Washington Post*, 16 June 2015.

12. Laura Barron-Lopez, "Scott Walker Open to Building a Wall Along Border With Canada," *Huffington Post*, 30 August 2015, http://www.huffington post.com/entry/scott-walker-canada-border-wall_55e308d8e4b0aec9f3538ee0 (accessed 30 October 2015).

13. Samuel P. Huntington, *Who Are We? The Challenges to America's National Identity* (New York: Simon & Schuster, 2004).

14. UNHCR, "UNHCR Calls for More Robust Search-and-Rescue Operation on Mediterranean," 12 February 2015, http://www.unhcr.org/54dc8dc59.html (accessed 30 October 2015).

15. Pew Research Center, "Mexican President Peña Nieto's Ratings Slip with Economic Reform," 26 August 2014, http://www.pewglobal.org/2014/08/26/mexican-president-pena-nietos-ratings-slip-with-economic-reform/ (accessed 30 October 2015).

16. Deborah Hardoon, *Wealth: Having It All and Wanting More* (Oxford: Oxfam International, 2015).

17. Dwight Eisenhower, "The Chance for Peace," 16 April 1953, http://www.eisenhower.archives.gov/all_about_ike/quotes.html (accessed 30 October 2015).

18. Stockholm International Peace Research Institute, *SIPRI Yearbook 2015: Armaments, Disarmament and International Security* (Oxford: Oxford University Press and SIPRI, 2015), http://www.sipri.org/yearbook/2015 (accessed 30 October 2015).

19. United Nations Development Programme, "Sustainable Development Goals Booklet," 28 September 2015, http://www.undp.org/content/undp/en/home/librarypage/corporate/sustainable-development-goals-booklet.html (accessed 30 October 2015).

RECOMMENDED READINGS

Adams, Francis, Satya Dev Gupta, and Kidane Mengisteab, eds. *Globalization and the Dilemmas of the State in the South.* New York: St. Martin's Press, 1999.

Adamson, Fiona. "Crossing Borders: International Migration and National Security." *International Security* 31, no. 1 (2006): 165–199.

Agbiboa, Daniel Egiegba. "Offsetting the Development Costs? Brain Drain and the Role of Training and Remittances." *Third World Quarterly* 33, no. 9 (2012): 1669–1683.

Aginam, Obijiofor. "Predatory Globalization." *Proceedings of the Annual Meeting/American Society of International Law* 104 (2010): 139–146.

Aman, Alfred C. "Introduction: Migration and Globalization." *Indiana Journal of Global Legal Studies* 2, no. 1 (1994): 1–4.

Amin, Samir. *Accumulation on a World Scale: A Critique of the Theory of Underdevelopment.* New York: Monthly Review, 1974.

Anderson, Benedict. *Imagined Communities: Reflections on the Origin and Spread of Nationalism.* London: Verso, 2006.

Antin, Mary. *The Promised Land.* Boston: Houghton Mifflin, 1969.

Appadurai, Arjun. *Globalization*. Durham, NC: Duke University Press, 2001.

———. *Modernity at Large: Cultural Dimensions of Globalization*. Minneapolis: University of Minnesota Press, 1996.

Armstrong, David. "Globalization and the Social State." *Review of International Studies* 24, no. 4 (1998): 461–478.

Axford, Barrie. *The Global System: Economics, Politics, and Culture*. New York: St. Martin's Press, 1995.

———. *Theories of Globalization*. Cambridge, UK: Polity, 2013.

Bacon, David. *Illegal People: How Globalization Creates Migration and Criminalizes Immigrants*. Boston: Beacon Press, 2008.

Bailyn, Bernard. *The Barbarous Years: The Peopling of British North America—The Conflict of Civilizations, 1600-1675*. New York: Alfred A. Knopf, 2012.

———. *The Peopling of British North America: An Introduction*. New York: Alfred A. Knopf, 1986.

Bailyn, Bernard, and Barbara DeWolfe. *Voyagers to the West: A Passage in the Peopling of America on the Eve of the Revolution*. New York: Alfred A. Knopf, 1986.

Bakewell, Oliver. *Migration and Development*. Cheltenham, UK: Edward Elgar, 2012.

Barber, Benjamin R. *Jihad vs. McWorld: Terrorism's Challenge to Democracy*. New York: Ballantine Books, 1996.

Beck, Ulrich. *What Is Globalization?* Cambridge, UK: Polity Press, 2000.

Berezin, Mabel, and Martin Schain. *Europe Without Borders: Remapping Territory, Citizenship, and Identity in a Transnational Age*. Baltimore: Johns Hopkins University Press, 2003.

Berger, Peter L., and Samuel P. Huntington. *Many Globalizations: Cultural Diversity in the Contemporary World*. Oxford: Oxford University Press, 2002.

Brady, David, Jason Beckfield, and Wei Zhao. "The Consequences of Economic Globalization for Affluent Democracies." *Annual Review of Sociology* 33 (2007): 313–334.

Brady, David, Martin Seeleib-Kaiser, and Jason Beckfield. "Economic Globalization and the Welfare State in Affluent Democracies, 1975–2001." *American Sociological Review* 70, no. 6 (2005): 921–948.

Braudel, Fernand. *The Mediterranean and the Mediterranean World in the Age of Philip II*. New York: Harper & Row, 1972.

Brenner, Robert. "The Origins of Capitalist Development: A Critique of Neo-Smithian Marxism." *New Left Review* 104 (1977): 25–92.

Brettell, Caroline, and James Frank Hollifield. *Migration Theory: Talking Across Disciplines*. New York: Routledge, 2008.

Brickner, Rachel K. *Migration, Globalization, and the State*. Basingstoke: Palgrave Macmillan, 2013.

Bryan, Lowell L., and Diana Farrell. *Market Unbound: Unleashing Global Capitalism*. New York: Wiley, 1996.

Castles, Stephen. *Ethnicity and Globalization: From Migrant Worker to Transnational Citizen.* London: Sage Publications, 2000.

——. "The Factors that Make and Unmake Migration Policies." *International Migration Review* 38, no. 3 (2004): 852–884.

——. "Migration and Community Formation under Conditions of Globalization." *International Migration Review* 36, no. 4 (2002): 1143–1168.

Castles, Stephen, and Mark J. Miller. *The Age of Migration.* New York: Guilford Press, 2003.

Connors, Michael. *The Race to the Intelligent State: Charting the Global Information Economy into the 21st Century.* Oxford: Capstone, 1997.

Conrad, Joseph, and Franklin Walker. *Heart of Darkness and the Secret Sharer: With an Introduction, Biographical Sketch, and a Selection of Background Materials and Commentaries by Franklin Walker.* New York: Bantam Books, 1971.

Cornelius, Wayne A. *Controlling Immigration: A Global Perspective.* Stanford, CA: Stanford University Press, 2004.

Cornwell, Grant Hermans, and Eve Walsh Stoddard. *Global Multiculturalism: Comparative Perspectives on Ethnicity, Race, and Nation.* Lanham, MD: Rowman & Littlefield Publishers, 2000.

Curtin, Philip D. *Cross-Cultural Trade in World History.* Cambridge: Cambridge University Press, 1984.

Dallmayr, Fred R. *Achieving Our World: Toward a Global and Plural Democracy.* Lanham, MD: Rowman & Littlefield Publishers, 2001.

Dasgupta, Samir, and Jan Nederveen Pieterse. *Politics of Globalization.* Los Angeles: Sage, 2009.

Diamond, Jared M. *Collapse: How Societies Choose to Fail or Succeed.* New York: Viking, 2005.

——. *Guns, Germs, and Steel: The Fates of Human Societies.* New York: Norton, 2005.

Diener, Alexander C., and Joshua Hagen. *Borderlines and Borderlands: Political Oddities at the Edge of the Nation-State.* Lanham, MD: Rowman & Littlefield Publishers, 2010.

Dinnerstein, Leonard, and David M. Reimers. *Ethnic Americans: A History of Immigration and Assimilation.* New York: Dodd, Mead, 1975.

Dinnerstein, Leonard, et al. *Natives and Strangers: Ethnic Groups and the Building of America.* New York: Oxford University Press, 1979.

Dreher, Axel, Martin Gassebner, and Lars-H. R. Siemers. "Globalization, Economic Freedom, and Human Rights." *Journal of Conflict Resolution* 56, no. 3 (2012): 516–546.

El Fisgón. *How to Succeed at Globalization: A Primer for Roadside Vendors.* New York: Metropolitan Books, 2004.

Erickson, Charlotte. *Invisible Immigrants: The Adaptation of English and Scottish Immigrants in Nineteenth-Century America.* Coral Gables: University of Miami Press, 1972.

Falk, Richard A. *Predatory Globalization: A Critique.* Cambridge: Polity Press, 1999.

Fanning, Bryan, and Ronaldo Munck. *Globalization, Migration and Social Transformation: Ireland in Europe and the World.* Farnham: Ashgate, 2011.

Fanon, Frantz. *The Wretched of the Earth.* Translated by Richard Philcox. New York: Grove Press, 1963.

Featherstone, Mike. *Global Culture: Nationalism, Globalization, and Modernity.* London: Sage Publications, 1990.

Felice, William F. *The Global New Deal: Economic and Social Human Rights in World Politics.* Lanham, MD: Rowman & Littlefield Publishers, 2010.

Ferguson, Niall. 2005. "Sinking Globalization." *Foreign Affairs* 84, no. 2 (2005): 64–77.

Fix, Michael. *Securing the Future: US Immigrant Integration Policy.* Washington, DC: Migration Policy Institute, 2007.

Foster, Robert John. *Coca-Globalization: Following Soft Drinks from New York to New Guinea.* New York: Palgrave Macmillan, 2008.

Frank, Andre Gunder. *ReOrient: Global Economy in the Asian Age.* Berkeley: University of California Press, 1998.

———. *World Accumulation, 1492–1789.* New York: Algora, 2007.

Freeman, Richard B. "People Flows in Globalization." *Journal of Economic Perspectives* 20, no. 2 (2006): 145–170.

Friedman, Jonathan. *Cultural Identity and Global Process.* London: Sage Publications, 1994.

Friedman, Thomas L. *The Lexus and the Olive Tree: Understanding Globalization.* New York: Farrar, Straus and Giroux, 1999.

———. *The World Is Flat: A Brief History of the Twenty-First Century.* New York: Farrar, Straus and Giroux, 2005.

Fukuyama, Francis. *The End of History and the Last Man.* New York: Free Press, 1992.

Gabaccia, Donna R., and Elizabeth Zanoni. "Transitions in Gender Ratios among International Migrants, 1820–1930." *Social Science History* 36, no. 2 (2012): 197–221.

Galeano, Eduardo. *Guatemala: Occupied Country.* New York: Monthly Review Press, 1969.

———. *Open Veins of Latin America: Five Centuries of the Pillage of a Continent.* New York: Monthly Review Press, 1973.

Gardiner Barber, Pauline. "The Ideal Immigrant? Gendered Class Subjects in Philippine-Canada Migration." *Third World Quarterly* 29, no. 7 (2008): 1265–1285.

Garrett, Geoffrey. "Globalization's Missing Middle." *Foreign Affairs* 83, no. 6 (2004): 84–96.

Gerdes, Louise I. *Immigration.* San Diego: Greenhaven Press, 2005.

Giddens, Anthony. *The Consequences of Modernity.* Stanford: Stanford University Press, 1990.

Givens, Terri E. *Immigration Policy and Security*. New York, London: Routledge, 2009.

Glazer, Nathan, and Daniel P. Moynihan. *Beyond the Melting Pot: The Negroes, Puerto Ricans, Jews, Italians, and Irish of New York City*. Cambridge, MA: M.I.T. Press, 1970.

Global Forum on Migration and Development, and Irena Omelaniuk. *Global Perspectives on Migration and Development: GFMD Puerto Vallarta and Beyond*. Dordrecht: Springer, 2012.

Goff, Patricia M. *Limits to Liberalization: Local Culture in a Global Marketplace*. Ithaca: Cornell University Press, 2007.

Göktürk, Deniz, David Gramling, and Anton Kaes. *Germany in Transit: Nation and Migration, 1955–2005*. Berkeley: University of California Press, 2007.

Goldin, Frances, Debby Smith, and Michael Steven Smith. *Imagine: Living in a Socialist USA*. New York: Harper Perennial, 2014.

Goodman, Gary L., and Jonathan T. Hiskey. "Exit without Leaving: Political Disengagement in High Migration Municipalities in Mexico." *Comparative Politics* 40, no. 2 (2008): 169–188.

Haas, Peter M. *Controversies in Globalization*. Washington, DC: CQ Press, 2013.

Handlin, Oscar. *The Newcomers: Negroes and Puerto Ricans in a Changing Metropolis*. Cambridge: Harvard University Press, 1959.

———. *The Uprooted*. Boston: Little, Brown, 1990.

Hannerz, Ulf. *Transnational Connections: Culture, People, Places*. London: Routledge, 1996.

Hansen, Marcus Lee, and Arthur M. Schlesinger. *The Atlantic Migration, 1607–1860: A History of the Continuing Settlement of the United States*. New York: Harper, 1961.

Harvey, David. *The Condition of Postmodernity: An Enquiry into the Origins of Cultural Change*. Oxford: Blackwell, 1990.

———. *Spaces of Global Capitalism*. London: Verso, 2006.

Hayden, Patrick, and Chamsy El-Ojeili. *Confronting Globalization: Humanity, Justice, and the Renewal of Politics*. New York: Palgrave Macmillan, 2005.

Hebron, Lui, and John F. Stack. *Globalization: Debunking the Myths*. Upper Saddle River, NJ: Pearson Prentice Hall, 2008.

Held, David. *Global Transformations: Politics, Economics and Culture*. Stanford: Stanford University Press, 1999.

Held, David, and Anthony G. McGrew. *The Global Transformations Reader: An Introduction to the Globalization Debate*. Malden, MA: Polity Press, 2000.

Held, David, Anthony McGrew, David Goldblatt, and Jonathan Perraton. "Globalization." *Global Governance* 5, no. 4 (1999): 483–496.

Higham, John. *Strangers in the Land: Patterns of American Nativism, 1860–1925*. New Brunswick, NJ: Rutgers University Press, 2002.

Hines, Colin. *Localization: A Global Manifesto*. London: Earthscan, 2000.

Hirsi Ali, Ayaan. *Nomad: From Islam to America: A Personal Journey through the Clash of Civilizations.* New York: Free Press, 2010.

Hirst, Paul Q., and Grahame Thompson. *Globalization in Question: The International Economy and the Possibilities of Governance.* Cambridge, UK: Polity, 1999.

Hobsbawm, E. J. *The Age of Empire, 1875–1914.* New York: Pantheon Books, 1987.

———. *The Age of Revolution, 1789–1848.* Cleveland: World Pub. Co., 1962.

———. *Industry and Empire: An Economic History of Britain Since 1750.* London: Weidenfeld & Nicolson, 1968.

———. *Nations and Nationalism Since 1780: Programme, Myth, Reality.* Cambridge: Cambridge University Press, 1992.

Hoffmann, Stanley. "Clash of Globalizations." *Foreign Affairs* 81, no. 4 (2002): 104–115.

Hollifield, James F. "The Emerging Migration State." *International Migration Review* 38, no. 3 (2004): 885–912.

Holmes, Seth. *Fresh Fruit, Broken Bodies: Migrant Farmworkers in the United States.* Berkeley: University of California Press, 2013.

Holton, Robert. *Globalization and the Nation-State.* New York: St. Martin's Press, 1998.

———. "Globalization's Cultural Consequences." *Annals of the American Academy of Political and Social Science* 570 (2000): 140–152.

Hopper, Paul. *Understanding Cultural Globalization.* Cambridge: Polity, 2007.

Huntington, Samuel P. *The Clash of Civilizations and the Remaking of World Order.* New York: Simon & Schuster, 1996.

———. *Who Are We? The Challenges to America's National Identity.* New York: Simon & Schuster, 2004.

Hutner, Gordon. *Immigrant Voices: Twenty-Four Narratives on Becoming an American.* New York: Signet Classic, 1999.

İçduygu, Ahmet, and E. Fuat Keyman. "Globalization, Security, and Migration: The Case of Turkey." *Global Governance* 6, no. 3 (2000): 383–398.

Inglehart, Ronald. *Modernization and Postmodernization: Cultural, Economic, and Political Change in Forty-Three Societies.* Princeton: Princeton University Press, 1997.

International Organization for Migration. *World Migration Report 2011: Communicating Effectively about Migration.* Geneva: International Organization for Migration, 2011.

———. *World Migration Report 2013: Migrant Well-being and Development.* Geneva: International Organization for Migration, 2013.

———. *World Migration Report 2015: Migrants and Cities.* Geneva: International Organization for Migration, 2015.

Jacoby, Tamar. *Reinventing the Melting Pot: The New Immigrants and What It Means to Be American.* New York: Basic Books, 2004.

Jameson, Fredric, and Masao Miyoshi. *The Cultures of Globalization.* Durham, NC: Duke University Press, 1998.

Johnson, Chalmers. *Blowback: The Costs and Consequences of American Empire.* New York: Henry Holt, 2001.

———. *Nemesis: The Last Days of the American Republic.* New York: Metropolitan Books, 2006.

———. *The Sorrows of Empire: Militarism, Secrecy, and the End of the Republic.* New York: Henry Holt, 2005.

Jones, R. J. Barry. *The World Turned Upside Down? Globalization and the Future of the State.* Manchester, UK: Manchester University Press, 2000.

Kacowicz, Arie M. "Globalization, Poverty, and the North-South Divide." *International Studies Review* 9, no. 4 (2007): 565–580.

Kelleher, Ann, and Laura F. Klein. *Global Perspectives: A Handbook for Understanding Global Issues.* Upper Saddle River, NJ: Prentice Hall, 2008.

Kennedy, John F. *A Nation of Immigrants.* New York: Harper and Row, 1964.

King, Anthony D. *Culture, Globalization, and the World-System: Contemporary Conditions for the Representation of Identity.* Minneapolis: University of Minnesota Press, 1997.

Klein, Naomi. *This Changes Everything: Capitalism Vs. The Climate.* New York: Simon & Schuster, 2014.

———. *The Shock Doctrine: The Rise of Disaster Capitalism.* New York: Metropolitan Books, 2007.

Korten, David C. *Globalizing Civil Society: Reclaiming Our Right to Power.* New York: Seven Stories Press, 1999.

———. *The Great Turning: From Empire to Earth Community.* San Francisco: Berrett-Koehler, 2006.

———. *The Post-Corporate World: Life After Capitalism.* San Francisco: Berrett-Koehler, 1999.

———. *When Corporations Rule the World.* 2nd ed. San Francisco: Berrett-Koehler, 2001.

Koser, Khalid. *International Migration: A Very Short Introduction.* Oxford: Oxford University Press, 2007.

Kraut, Alan M. *The Huddled Masses: The Immigrant in American Society, 1880–1921.* Arlington Heights, IL: Harlan Davidson, 1982.

Larner, Wendy, and William Walters. "Globalization as Governmentality." *Alternatives: Global, Local, Political* 29, no. 5 (2004): 495–514.

Lechner, Frank, and John Boli. *The Globalization Reader.* Malden, MA: Blackwell, 2004.

Legomsky, Stephen H. *Immigration and Refugee Law and Policy.* Westbury, NY: Foundation Press, 1997.

LeMay, Michael C. *Anatomy of a Public Policy: The Reform of Contemporary American Immigration Law.* Westport, CT: Praeger, 1994.

Lewis, Bernard. *What Went Wrong? The Clash between Islam and Modernity in the Middle East.* New York: Perennial, 2003.

López-Córdova, J. Ernesto. *Globalization, Migration and Development: The Role of Mexican Migrant Remittances.* Buenos Aires: Institute for the Integration of Latin America and the Caribbean, 2006.

Luttwak, Edward. *Turbo-Capitalism: Winners and Losers in the Global Economy.* New York: Harper, 1999.

Malthus, T. R., and Geoffrey Gilbert. *An Essay on the Principle of Population.* Oxford: Oxford University Press, 2008.

Manning, Patrick. *Migration in World History.* New York: Routledge, 2005.

Mansbach, Richard W., and Edward Rhodes. *Introducing Globalization: Analysis and Readings.* Los Angeles: Sage, 2013.

Martiniello, Marco, and Jan Rath. *An Introduction to International Migration Studies: European Perspectives.* Amsterdam: Amsterdam University Press, 2012.

Massey, Douglas S. *Worlds in Motion: Understanding International Migration at the End of the Millennium.* Oxford: Clarendon Press, 2005.

Mazlish, Bruce. "A Tour of Globalization." *Indiana Journal of Global Legal Studies* 7, no. 1 (1999): 5–16.

McKeown, Adam. "Global Migration 1846–1940." *Journal of World History* 15, no. 2 (2004): 155–189.

McLuhan, Marshall. *The Gutenberg Galaxy: The Making of Typographic Man.* London: Routledge & Kegaul, 1962.

Messina, Anthony M., and Gallya Lahav. *The Migration Reader: Exploring Politics and Policy.* Boulder, CO: Lynne Rienner Publishers, 2006.

Miller, Daniel, *Worlds Apart: Modernity through the Prism of the Local.* London: Routledge, 1995.

Mills, Nicolaus. *Arguing Immigration: The Debate Over the Changing Face of America.* New York: Simon & Schuster, 1994.

Mittelman, James H. *Globalization: Critical Reflections.* Boulder, CO: Lynne Rienner Publishers, 1996.

Mobasher, Mohsen M., and Mahmoud Sadri. *Migration, Globalization, and Ethnic Relations: An Interdisciplinary Approach.* Upper Saddle River, NJ: Pearson, 2004.

Morris, Lydia. "Globalization, Migration and the Nation-State: The Path to a Post-National Europe?" *British Journal of Sociology* 48, no. 2 (1997): 192–209.

Moses, Jonathon W. "Exit, Vote and Sovereignty: Migration, States and Globalization." *Review of International Political Economy* 12, no. 1 (2005): 53–77.

Munck, Ronaldo. *Globalisation and Migration: New Issues, New Politics.* London: Routledge, 2009.

———. "Globalisation, Governance and Migration: An Introduction." *Third World Quarterly* 29, no. 7 (2008): 1227–1246.

Naím, Moisés. "Globalization." *Foreign Policy* 171 (2009): 28–34.

Naples, Nancy A., and Jennifer Bickham Méndez. *Border Politics: Social Movements, Collective Identities, and Globalization*. New York: New York University Press, 2014.

Ngai, Mae M., and Jon Gjerde. *Major Problems in American Immigration History: Documents and Essays*. Boston, MA: Wadsworth, 2013.

Ōmae, Ken'ichi. *The Borderless World: Power and Strategy in the Interlinked Economy*. New York: Harper, 1990.

———. *The End of the Nation State: The Rise of Regional Economies*. New York: Free Press, 1995.

———. *The Next Global Stage: Challenges and Opportunities in Our Borderless World*. Upper Saddle River, NJ: Wharton School Pub., 2005.

Organisation for Economic Co-operation and Development. *Globalisation, Migration, and Development*. Paris: OECD, 2000.

Orozco, Manuel. "Globalization and Migration: The Impact of Family Remittances in Latin America." *Latin American Politics and Society* 44, no. 2 (2002): 41–66.

Panitch, Leo, and Sam Gindin. *The Making of Global Capitalism: The Political Economy of American Empire*. London: Verso, 2012.

Papastergiadis, Nikos. *The Turbulence of Migration: Globalization, Deterritorialization, and Hybridity*. Cambridge, UK: Polity Press, 2000.

Payne, Richard J. *Global Issues: Politics, Economics, and Culture*. New York: Pearson Longman, 2009.

Pellerin, Hélène. "Global Restructuring in the World Economy and Migration: The Globalization of Migration Dynamics." *International Journal* 48, no. 2 (1993): 240–254.

Perz, Stephen G. "The Rural Exodus in the Context of Economic Crisis, Globalization and Reform in Brazil." *International Migration Review* 34, no. 3 (2000): 842–881.

Pieterse, Jan Nederveen. *Globalization or Empire?* New York: Routledge, 2004.

Piper, Nicola. "Feminisation of Migration and the Social Dimensions of Development: The Asian Case." *Third World Quarterly* 29, no. 7 (2008): 1287–1303.

Portes, Alejandro, and John Walton. *Labor, Class, and the International System*. New York: Academic Press, 1981.

Portes, Alejandro, and Rubén G. Rumbaut. *Immigrant America: A Portrait*. Berkeley; Los Angeles; London: University of California Press, 2006.

Prazniak, Roxann, and Arif Dirlik. *Places and Politics in an Age of Globalization*. Lanham, MD: Rowman & Littlefield Publishers, 2001.

Quintero-Rivera, Ángel G. "Cultural Struggles for Hegemony: Salsa, Migration, and Globalization." *Latin American Perspectives: A Journal of Capitalism and Socialism* 38, no. 2 (2011): 58–70.

Reich, Robert B. *Saving Capitalism: For the Many, Not the Few*. New York: Alfred A. Knopf, 2015.

Ribas-Mateos, Natalia. *The Mediterranean in the Age of Globalization: Migration, Welfare & Borders*. New Brunswick, NJ: Transaction Publishers, 2005.

Robbins, Richard Howard. *Global Problems and the Culture of Capitalism*. Boston: Allyn & Bacon, 2008.

Robertson, Roland. *Globalization: Social Theory and Global Culture*. London: Sage, 1992.

Rosenau, James N. *Distant Proximities: Dynamics Beyond Globalization*. Princeton, NJ: Princeton University Press, 2003.

Rupert, Mark, and M. Scott Solomon. *Globalization and International Political Economy: The Politics of Alternative Futures*. Lanham, MD: Rowman & Littlefield Publishers, 2006.

Samers, Michael. "'Globalization,' the Geopolitical Economy of Migration and the 'Spatial Vent.'" *Review of International Political Economy* 6, no. 2 (1999): 166–199.

Sanderson, Matthew R., and Jeffrey Kentor. "Globalization, Development and International Migration: A Cross-National Analysis of Less-Developed Countries, 1970–2000." *Social Forces* 88, no. 1 (2009): 301–336.

Sassen, Saskia. *The Global City: New York, London, Tokyo*. Princeton, NJ: Princeton University Press, 2001.

———. *Globalization and Its Discontents*. New York: New Press, 1998.

Schaeffer, Robert K. *Understanding Globalization: The Social Consequences of Political, Economic, and Environmental Change*. Lanham, MD: Rowman & Littlefield Publishers, 2009.

Schain, Martin. *The Politics of Immigration in France, Britain, and the United States: A Comparative Study*. New York: Palgrave Macmillan, 2008.

Scholte, Jan Aart. *Globalization: A Critical Introduction*. New York: St. Martin's Press, 2000.

Sernau, Scott. *Global Problems: The Search for Equity, Peace, and Sustainability*. Boston: Pearson, 2009.

Singer, Peter. *One World: The Ethics of Globalization*. New Haven: Yale University Press, 2002.

Sinke, Suzanne M. "Gender and Migration: Historical Perspectives." *International Migration Review* 40, no. 1 (2006): 82–103.

Smith, Adam, and Edwin Cannan. *The Wealth of Nations*. New York: Modern Library, 2000.

Smith, Jackie. *Global Democracy and the World Social Forums*. Boulder, CO: Paradigm Publishers, 2007.

Snarr, Michael T., and Neil Snarr. *Introducing Global Issues*. Boulder, CO: Lynne Rienner Publishers, 2012.

Snethen, John D. "The Evolution of Sovereignty and Citizenship in Western Europe: Implications for Migration and Globalization." *Indiana Journal of Global Legal Studies* 8, no. 1 (2000): 223–249.

Solimano, Andrés. *International Migration in the Age of Crisis and Globalization: Historical and Recent Experiences*. New York: Cambridge University Press, 2010.

Soros, George. *George Soros on Globalization*. New York: Public Affairs, 2002.

Sowell, Thomas. *Migrations and Cultures: A World View*. New York: Basic Books, 1996.

Stalker, Peter. *Workers Without Frontiers: The Impact of Globalization on International Migration*. Boulder, CO: Lynne Rienner Publishers, 2000.

Steger, Manfred B. *Globalization*. New York: Sterling Publishing Co. Inc., 2010.

———. *Globalization: A Very Short Introduction*. Oxford: Oxford University Press, 2003.

———. *Globalization and Culture*. Cheltenham, UK: Edward Elgar, 2012.

———. *Globalization: The Greatest Hits, a Global Studies Reader*. Boulder, CO: Paradigm Publishers, 2010.

———. *The Rise of the Global Imaginary: Political Ideologies from the French Revolution to the Global War on Terror*. Oxford: Oxford University Press, 2008.

Stiglitz, Joseph E. *Globalization and Its Discontents*. New York: W.W. Norton, 2002.

———. *The Great Divide: Unequal Societies and What We Can Do About Them*. New York: W.W. Norton & Company, 2015.

———. *The Price of Inequality: How Today's Divided Society Endangers Our Future*. New York: W.W. Norton & Company, 2012.

Talani, Leila Simona. *From Egypt to Europe: Globalisation and Migration Across the Mediterranean*. London: Tauris Academic Studies, 2010.

Talbott, Strobe. *The Great Experiment: The Story of Ancient Empires, Modern States, and the Quest for a Global Nation*. New York: Simon & Schuster, 2008.

Thurow, Lester C. *The Future of Capitalism: How Today's Economic Forces Shape Tomorrow's World*. New York: William Morrow, 1996.

Tilly, Charles. *Durable Inequality*. Berkeley: University of California Press, 1998.

———. *Identities, Boundaries, and Social Ties*. Boulder, CO: Paradigm Publishers, 2005.

United Nations High Commissioner for Refugees. *World at War: UNHCR Global Trends*. Geneva: UNHCR, 2015.

United Nations Statistics Division. *Recommendations on Statistics of International Migration, Revision 1*. New York: United Nations, 1998.

Veseth, Michael. *Globaloney 2.0: The Crash of 2008 and the Future of Globalization*. Lanham, MD: Rowman & Littlefield Publishers, 2010.

Wallerstein, Immanuel. *The Decline of American Power: The U.S. In a Chaotic World*. New York: New Press, 2003.

———. *Does Capitalism Have a Future?* Oxford: Oxford University Press, 2013.

———. *Historical Capitalism with Capitalist Civilization*. London: Verso, 2011.

———. *The Modern World-System I: Capitalist Agriculture and the Origins of the European World-Economy in the Sixteenth Century*. Berkeley: University of California, 2011.

———. *The Modern World-System II: Mercantilism and the Consolidation of the European World-Economy, 1600–1750.* Berkeley: University of California, 2011.

———. *The Modern World-System III: The Second Era of Great Expansion of the Capitalist World-Economy, 1730s–1840s.* Berkeley: University of California, 2011.

———. *The Modern World-System IV: Centrist Liberalism Triumphant, 1789–1914.* Berkeley: University of California, 2011.

———. *The Modern World-System in the Longue Durée.* Boulder, CO: Paradigm Publishers, 2004.

———. *World-Systems Analysis: An Introduction.* Durham, NC: Duke University Press, 2004.

Waters, Malcolm. *Globalization.* London: Routledge, 1995.

Weatherford, Jack. *Genghis Khan and the Making of the Modern World.* New York: Crown, 2004.

Wermuth, Laurie Ann. *Global Inequality and Human Needs: Health and Illness in an Increasingly Unequal World.* Boston, MA: Allyn and Bacon, 2003.

Wickramasekara, Piyasiri. "Globalisation, International Labour Migration and the Rights of Migrant Workers." *Third World Quarterly* 29, no. 7 (2008): 1247–1264.

Wolf, Martin. *Why Globalization Works.* New Haven: Yale University Press, 2004.

Zakaria, Fareed. *The Post-American World.* New York: W.W. Norton, 2008.

Zolberg, Aristide R. *A Nation by Design: Immigration Policy in the Fashioning of America.* Cambridge, MA: Harvard University Press, 2008.

INDEX

Page references for figures are italicized.

ABOUT THE AUTHO

Eliot Dickinson is professor of politics and peace studies at We Oregon University. He earned a PhD in political science from Pu University and worked at both the University of the Witwatersrar South Africa and Hope College in Michigan before moving to Ore His areas of expertise include comparative politics, international tions, and political theory. He is author of the book *Copts in Mic* (Michigan State University Press, 2008) and a number of article book chapters on South African politics, Austrian politics, and Ge immigration policy.